Famous Colonial Houses

MONTICELLO

"Mr. Jefferson," said one of Rochambeau's aides, "is the first American who has consulted the fine arts to know how he should shelter himself from the weather." With no continental travel for background, with only the meager pictorial record of the period to draw upon, he somehow responded instantly to the simplicity and useful beauty of the classics, and translated it to his castle.

Famous Colonial Houses

By

Paul M. Hollister

Illustrated by

James Preston

With an Introduction by

Julian Street

Ross & Perry, Inc.
Washington, D.C.

Copyright 1921, David McKay Company
Reprinted by Ross & Perry, Inc. 2002
© Ross & Perry, Inc. 2002 on new material. All rights reserved.

Protected under the Berne Convention.

Printed in The United States of America

Ross & Perry, Inc. Publishers
216 G St., N.E.
Washington, D.C. 20002
Telephone (202) 675-8300
Facsimile (202) 675-8400
info@RossPerry.com

SAN 253-8555

Library of Congress Control Number: 2002106274
http://www.rossperry.com

ISBN 1-932080-36-8

Book Cover designed by Sapna. sapna@rossperry.com

❊ The paper used in this publication meets the requirements for permanence established by the American National Standard for Information Sciences "Permanence of Paper for Printed Library Materials" (ANSI Z39.48-1984).

All rights reserved. No copyrighted part of this publication may be reproduced, stored in a retrieval system, or transmitted, in any form or by any means, electronic, photocopying, recording, or otherwise, without the prior written permission of the publisher.

TO

MARION

List of Illustrations

Monticello	*Frontispiece.*
	Facing Page
The Haunted House, New Orleans	28
Doughoregan Manor	42
The Jumel Mansion	54
Mount Vernon	68
The Quincy Homestead	82
The Timothy Dexter Mansion	94
The Kendall House	106
The Longfellow House	120
Cliveden	134
The Wentworth Mansion	144
The Pringle House	158

Foreword

THERE is no bibliography in this book. I confess freely to a snapping-up of ill-considered trifles where I found them. Those that rang true are here, those that proved false upon closer examination are not. Some were gifts, some purchases, some thefts—the latter are now shamelessly confessed, on the plea that as a citizen I have the right of eminent domain to the story of my country. I cannot put the volume out to shift for itself without blanket acknowledgment of the generosity of the people who put me in the way of finding reliable information. Several of them are the owners of the houses; some of them have even read this manuscript.

—Boston, September, 1921.

INTRODUCTION

AS I read in Mr. Hollister's chapter on Mount Vernon of Washington's long absence from the home he loved and of the eagerness with which he returned to it after the tumultuous years of the Revolutionary War, I was caught by the fancy that lovers of books have recently gone through a somewhat parallel experience. Dragged away by the Great War from the books they cared for, plunged into continual war reading, they now find, to their infinite relief, that they are getting home again—back to Mount Vernon, as it were. And it seems to me the change could not better be exemplified than in this charming, gentle book of Famous Colonial Houses.

While we were fighting to preserve the heritage and the traditions left us by Washington, Jefferson, Carroll of Carrollton, and other great figures of their time, whom we find in these pages, we were too busily engaged to give much thought to the origins of the things we fought to save. Not that the forefathers of the nation were forgotten, but that historic men were, in that time of stress, overshadowed by historic principles laid down by them. We put them aside tenderly, as books are put aside when the sword is taken up. Yet now that we have vindicated in battle the freedom that they gave us, we find them more than ever with us. For a just war fought through to victory sheds glory not only upon the men who fought it and the nation for which they fought, but also upon the nation's ancient heroes, whose stature is increased with that of their country. Wherefore this book, telling tales of old houses in which early American history was made, and of

INTRODUCTION

men who made the houses and the history, is even more welcome today than it would have been before the Great War.

It is welcome, too, for another partially extrinsic reason.

In the face of mutterings of anarchy—that Russian importation which is so much less satisfactory than the caviar—there is reassurance in these sturdy calm old mansions which are the monuments of the sturdy calm old patriots who raised them—men having a rare sense of proportion which they exercised not only in building their houses but in building the nation on lines equally clean, sound and beautiful. Fancy a shaggy Bolshevik, his mouth full of broken English, his head full of sophistry, and his heart full of greed for the possessions of others, being led up Mount Vernon, Monticello or Doughoregan Manor! Could any contrast make a picture more grotesque? Could there be conceived a background more serenely sane, more perfectly American, against which to display the distortion of this foreign madness? Every stone and brick and timber of such houses preaches a sermon on Americanism.

It is a sermon not only for aliens, but for all of us. We should all see these houses, or if we cannot see them, we should know them as some of them are made known to us in this book. Our land is a better land for having them within its borders, and we will be better citizens for an acquaintance with them.

The day on which I went to Monticello was beautiful, yet, save my companion, no one else was there. I wonder how many of the politicians who, with the *vox humana* stop pulled out, acclaim the name of Jefferson as founder of the Democratic Party, have made the short pilgrimage from Washington to Charlottesville to visit the house he lived in and the grave where he is buried.

In curious contrast to the large investment of the nation in National

INTRODUCTION

Parks, is its apparent indifference in the matter of the homes of its historic figures. Not one of the houses dealt with by Mr. Hollister in this book is the property of the nation. Two of them are, to be sure, houses which, though their story is interesting, are not involved with national history; and some of the others are not of sufficient importance, from the purely historical point of view, to make them national monuments of the first order. But two are, on the other hand, the homes of early presidents, and neither of these is owned by the nation. For all practical purposes Mount Vernon is as free to the public as though the nation did own it, but the fact remains that the title to it is vested in a society; while as for Monticello, it is owned by a private individual, not a descendant of Jefferson, into whose hands it came by inheritance from a forebear said to have secured it in a not too creditable way. It is difficult to understand why the State of Virginia or the Nation has not bought the place, which, I am told, the owner has declared his willingness to part with—at a price.

The census of the twelve houses described and pictured in this book is worth completing. One, Mount Vernon, is, as I have said, owned by an organization of patriotic women; two are owned by their municipalities and are cared for by patriotic organizations; one only is the home of a lineal descendant and namesake of the builder—though three others belong to persons having in their veins blood of the first masters of their houses. And one—a most interesting, but not historic house—is a poor battered tenement. Seven of the houses are situated in Northern States, one in a Border State, and four are in the South. The builders of two of the houses, the first and third Presidents of the United States, are buried on the grounds nearby, and in one case the builder is buried under the chancel of a private chapel, a part of the house itself.

INTRODUCTION

These historic houses may well be regarded as taking the place with us of the crown jewels of an empire. I am thankful to have seen eight of the twelve. For, like one of Goldsmith's characters, "I love everything that's old—old friends, old times, old manors, old books, old wine."

Therefore I find myself particularly pleased at being associated with this book, though in so slight a way. The two men who created it—for in this case the author and the artist surely stand on equal footing—are my old friends. Obviously, the book is one of old times and old manors, and if that does not make it an old book, what could? Only the old wine is lacking to complete the quintet. And even that may some day be accessible again. Who knows?

—*Julian Street.*

NORFOLK, CONN.,
September, 1921.

MONTICELLO

Famous Colonial Houses

MONTICELLO

IN Thomas Jefferson's boyhood imagination the hill had seemed to climb like Jack's beanstalk to the infinite clouds. The view from his Father's dooryard across the Rivanna registered each day through the clear lenses of his eyes upon the sensitive plate of his memory, and so upon his heart. As a lad he staged mental melodrama upon its symmetrical slopes and built an air-castle upon its summit. Every engagement of Caesar's conquests, every adventure of the pious Aeneas found on Monticello a proper setting. If his schoolbooks had not been burned in the fire at Shadwell we might expect to find, on the margins of his Horace, a sketch of the castle of his dream, for Jefferson drew rather well and probably sketched just as well during study hour as any other boy of his age.

He was nineteen when his dream promised to materialize. That summer and the next, when he was at home for the long holiday, he would cross the Rivanna in his canoe and climb the slope to see how the workmen were getting on with the levelling for his castle. As the boy had grown towards manhood the hill no longer towered into the skies, but whatever the picture lost in size, it gained in rich associations. It was still *his* mountain: *Monticello*—"little mountain"—he called it. "Our own dear Monticello, where Nature has spread such a rich mantle under the eye, mountains, forests, rocks, rivers. There is a mountain there in the opposite direction of the afternoon's sun, the valley between which and Monticello is five hundred feet deep.

FAMOUS COLONIAL HOUSES

. . . How sublime to look down upon the workhouse of Nature, to see her clouds, hail, snow, rain, thunder, all fabricated at our feet."

In all weathers, under all trials, his heart took refuge on the hill. He was admitted to the bar in 1767, made headway in his profession, and was sent to the House of Burgesses, honors which only quickened his impatient accomplishment, and his desire for a home upon his mountain. In 1769 its plans were ready, and work began. Thirty years later it was finished. During those years he wrote his country's bill of divorce from her harsh proprietor, and was nearly captured at Monticello by British raiders. Monticello saw him ride down the winding road as a Burgess, to ride up again as a member of the Continental Congress; honored him as Governor of Virginia, and waved him Godspeed as he left to succeed Benjamin Franklin as envoy to France; hailed him home as Washington's secretary of state, and then reluctantly surrendered him to eight years in a new White House that stood in a sandy wilderness somewhere down on the banks of the Potomac. But when his active life was done, after he had not only written the Declaration of Independence but prosecuted it, added half a continent to its jurisdiction, and administered the doctrine that all men are created free and equal, he came back to the mountain of his memory to gaze down upon the workhouse of Nature.

"While it is too much to say," writes Julian Street, "that one would recognize it as the house of the writer of the Declaration, it is not too much to say, that once one does know it, one can trace a clear affinity resulting from a common origin—an affinity much more apparent, by the way, than can be traced between the work of Michelangelo on St. Peter's at Rome, on the ceiling of the Sistine Chapel, and in his 'David.'

"The introductory paragraph to the Declaration ascends into the body of the document as gracefully as the wide flights of easy steps ascend to the doors of Monticello; the long and beautifully balanced paragraph which follows, building word upon word and sentence upon sentence into a central statement, has a form as definite and graceful as that of the finely proportioned house; the numbered paragraphs which follow, setting forth separate details, are like rooms within the house, and—I have just come upon the coincidence with a pleasant start such as might be felt by the discoverer of some complex and important cipher—as there are twenty-seven of the numbered paragraphs in the Declaration, so there are twenty-seven rooms in Monticello. Last of all there are two little phrases in the Declaration (the phrases stating that we shall hold our British brethren in future as we hold the rest of mankind—'enemies in war; in peace, friends'), which I would liken to the small twin buildings, one of them Jefferson's office, the other that of the overseer, which stand on either side of the lawn at Monticello, at some distance from the house."

The house which inspired and witnessed the activities of so prominent a figure could hardly lack distinction, and this, of course, Monticello has. What is more, Monticello is a monument of technical architecture which attracts the eager attention of every student of American domestic building. The question they all ask, and the question that cannot be answered, is: "Where could this farmer-lawyer boy have got his expert training in architecture?" His library might have given us a clue, but it was burned at Shadwell in 1770. We know he felt this loss acutely, for, next to his house, Jefferson loved his books. He asked anxiously of their fate. An old slave answered: "All burnt, my young master, all burnt. But never mind, sir"—and his wrinkled face broke into a broad smile—"we saved your old fiddle!" The new house at Monticello was even then far enough along to take in his mother's family, evicted by the fire. The building continued. It was slow work, on an extensive plan.

"Mr. Jefferson," said one of Rochambeau's aides later, "is the first American who has consulted the fine arts to know how he should shelter himself from the weather." With no continental travel for background, with only the meagre pictorial record of the period to draw upon, he somehow responded instantly to the simplicity and useful beauty of the classic, and translated it to his castle. By the Greeks, for example, it was thought improper that a roof should indicate anything but a glorification of the heavens; the idea that human feet might be walking on the upper side of a ceiling was sacrilege. This (and other more practical engineering reasons) dictated single-story buildings. Jefferson's eye for balance caught the pictorial advantages of one-story construction, but he needed two stories for Monticello, and by his shrewd planning both the pure classic tradition and pure American comfort were reconciled.

At the end of a broad lawn, in full relief against the distant sky, stands a red brick house with a clean, tall portico. The four gleaming pillars stand guard like peace-time sentinels. A white balustrade runs along the eaves of the building, tempering the irregularities in the roof except where the smooth curve of a dome rises above the center. The feeling is classic, and so suggests a single story, and the length of the lofty windows flanking the portico seems to confirm the impression that a single frame has been carried the full height of the house. Closer examination, however, of the irregularities just remarked in the roof reveals them as the gabled windows of an upper story. In cold, unprofessional analysis, the compromise sounds thoroughly impractical. Just the contrary is true, for Jefferson took up every challenging problem with enthusiasm, and applied

MONTICELLO

to its solution a sure sense of balance and a hearty appetite for detail.

Indoors the one-story tradition is quite as respectfully acknowledged, and as cleverly evaded. The entrance hall is a lofty room of great dignity, almost so good that a job-lot of Victorian furniture has not damaged its appearance, and unquestionably so good that even the most critical architectural eye will not take offense at a balcony which travels three of its sides. There is the balcony, but where, inquires your classic eye, are the stairs? Concealed in a passage, where they cannot break the form of the hall from which visitors are to gain their first impression of the interior.

If the visitor in Jefferson's day went further, as his uniform hospitality required, he may have noticed as he passed to the drawing-room that the portal between the two rooms had two pairs of doors. There was a definite reason for them: the wall must be heavy to support the octagon in which the drawing-room was situated, and over which rose the dome. A single pair of doors would have made an ugly recess in either room. Two sets of doors finished both rooms correctly, but presented just twice as many nice problems of treatment. So the first set was made of heavily paneled wood, and might be folded back into an invisible pocket in the passage; the second set was a pair of light casements, and if the visitor were to press a spring on either one, both would close by a mechanism concealed overhead.

Throughout the building there were ingenious touches which disclosed beneath their first impression of simple luxurious comfort the patient scheming of the builder. The drawing-room was octagonal in order that five windows might frame clear vistas in as many directions across the sweeping valleys to the horizon. The floor there is of squares of cherry wood, each with a liberal border of contrasting beech; both woods were laid only after Jefferson had made painstaking experiment in the color and in the wearing and joining qualities of various kinds of flooring. The same note of formality which one feels in the Pringle house of Charleston as he passes from room to room through heavily pedimented doorways is sounded at Monticello; but where Miles Brewton, in his Charleston house, held strictly to the "egg-and-dart" of the classic mode, Thomas Jefferson embellished the friezes above the doors of his drawing-room with a motive of tomahawks, scalping knives and rosettes! He feared that the dining-room, with only two southerly windows for ventilation, might become close toward the end of a long meal, so he gave a slight dome-like concavity to the ceiling, and at its focal center concealed under a grille the intake of a ventilator which leads up through the roof. He built a recess for the sideboard with the double effect of preserving the lines of the apartment and of displaying a handsome piece of furniture to its best advantage. An exquisite Adam mantel, with Wedgwood panels, stands between two of the windows, and you would never guess that in one of its sides is a door, and behind that door a dumbwaiter leading from the service rooms below. He wanted his body-servant's room conveniently near his own, so a staircase to the valet's quarters ascends through a spacious closet off the master's chamber. None of the liaison between art and artifice would be remarkable today, perhaps. There are modern houses as honestly built as men of taste can plan and men of wealth can buy, to match Touraine for splendor, Italy for gilt, a highly organized railway terminal for convenience and Sybaris for comfort. But given the workmanship, the materials and the engineering of any period in our domestic architecture, Monticello challenges them all to show a better plan.

Long balustraded walks reach out to right and left from the

house. Someone has likened them to two friendly outstretched arms, holding in each hand not a jewel, but a dainty summer-house. They are more than decorative promenades—each is the roof of a subterranean arcade, passing from the main building to the servants' quarters. All of the strictly domestic affairs were in the cellar-story, made habitable by the fact that it was just a step down the hillside, and made by no means the least interesting portion of the building by further evidence of Jefferson's genius. It is a veritable catacomb. He built there a kitchen ventilated by long ducts which carried cooking odors to distant outlets; he built cisterns, a large carriage court, cold-rooms, bins for fruits, and wood, and cider; servants' quarters so placed that they were cool in summer and warm in winter. Like Mount Vernon, and every other colonial estate of any size, Monticello was a self-maintaining establishment, which supported the labor of several trades. But the tailor-shop, the distillery, the smithy, the dye-house, the cobblery, the weaver's shop—all were set apart from the main house and concealed from the general eye. Later architects thought enough of the treatment of the arcade passages to the servants' quarters to copy them for the subterranean barracks at Fortress Monroe.

One wonders where Thomas Jefferson found the time for all this labor and supervision. The answer must be that his house was his one consuming avocation. It is almost a truism that the men upon whom are made the heaviest demands find time to invite the greatest number of demands. As Roosevelt loved his natural history, and made affectionate excursions into botany, so Jefferson knew every tree and shrub on his estate, and watched over it. Each week during his presidency a letter was despatched from the White House to Captain Bacon, his overseer in charge, directing transplanting, grading, repairs, improvements. Many of the workmen on the estate were men whom he himself had trained in their crafts. Some were slaves, whom he later freed to practise the trades he had given them. Before he had stone cut and measured for the building he tested the stone; he weathered various woods; he made experiments in brick-laying which in some cases led him to strange conclusions, but which, like everything else he undertook about the building, had practical reasoning behind them. And yet, during all the patient hours he spent in drafting and directing, the miles he walked in surveying and landscaping, he never let the cloud of details eclipse the artist's star.

Jefferson has been much idolized for his directness, his logic, his practicality. He undoubtedly gave the country what today would be termed "a good business administration." It is tempting to leave him to posterity with that reputation, and with the Louisiana Purchase as its brightest testimonial, the shrewdest real estate deal in our history. But Monticello is so obviously the product of an artist and a scholar that we learn with no hint of damage to his commoner reputation that the man who had spent his life upon this estate had also spent much more money than he possessed; that his generosity approached extravagance; that his library of some seven thousand volumes, the best then in America, was sold after his death to the government (to replace the library the British destroyed at Washington in 1814) because it had to be sold to meet his debts; and that Monticello itself finally passed out of the hands of his family. With Jefferson gone Monticello could never be wholly itself again. It must stand always as the finest exposition of the heart of the artist who conceived the plan for the University of Virginia at Monticello's skirts, who found when he visited Nîmes a Roman Temple which so fascinated him that he said the peasants thought him a mad Englishman contemplating suicide in its ruins, who copied that same temple for the Capitol of Richmond, and who wrote to a Paris acquaintance: "Here I am gazing whole hours at the *Maison Quarrée* like a lover at his mistress."

When Jefferson died he was buried on the estate. An army of human rodents came to see to his grave and to nibble away most of the memorial shaft, and it was only through the persistent efforts of his grand-daughter, Miss Randolph, that the United States stepped in and restored it. Meanwhile the estate had been sold under questionable circumstances to a Captain Uriah Levy. In justice to him be it said that he felt the responsibility of his charge, and bequeathed it at his death to the people of the United States. But the Supreme Court decreed that this definition was too vague, and after a prolonged debate among Levy's heirs, his nephew, Jefferson Levy, acquired for $10,500 the title to the buildings and 218 acres of the little mountain.

Sporadic efforts have been made to buy the estate and rescue it from the casual upkeep which is carrying Monticello steadily towards the shadows of oblivion; one such movement, under the leadership of Mrs. Martin W. Littleton, bade fair to succeed, and there were patriotic women ready to assume its care as they have so admirably done at Mount Vernon. The Governor of Virginia is silent on the subject, and the Wilson government, which owed more perhaps to Jefferson than to any other single preceptor, was otherwise engaged. With the return of peace the renewal of the project is, to say the least, appropriate. Whether it contains an appeal to the honor of citizenship in a nation in which all men are free and equal, is for its citizens—and one of them is the owner—to decide.

The Haunted House,
New Orleans

THE HAUNTED HOUSE

That April-day crowd returned to Hospital and Royal Streets and sacked the house from hall to belvedere, ripped down silk curtains, slashed paintings, wrenched out chandeliers, dug up two skeletons from the courtyard, pitched Madame Lalaurie's precious possessions out of windows and made bonfire of the wreckage in the street. Nor when inside the stout old walls a new and finer residence was built in cheerful defiance of the ghost, could the spirit of tragedy be banished.

The Haunted House, New Orleans

FAR down in the *vieux carré*, the old French quarter of New Orleans, where Hospital Street meets Royal, the drone of the modern city at work comes faintly through the morning air. Back yonder, above Canal Street, there are motor trucks, profanity and clangor; here there is hardly a street-car, and if you hear loud voices they are filtered through the shutters of a shabby dwelling where a hopeful candidate for the Opera is practising her topmost. The old French Opera House, the scene of Patti's debut, departed this life only last year—a gay life, marked by amours and appointments, triumphs and disappointments, dances and duels. Presently there will be gaps in the circle of musicians who always settle about the focal point of an opera house, and you will hear no more the manifold outpourings of their several souls, throats and fiddles.

Their passing will deepen the twilight of an antiquity which New Orleans has cherished with more sympathy than all the rest of our American cities. Rigid modern buildings with Louis XVI fronts and O'Shaughnessy backs will rear their ventilators, tanks and pent-houses where, once upon a time, warm walls and climbing cupolas, odd contours and vine-like wrought-iron railings melted into a strangely complex and beautiful composition. Even now, as the fitful trolley-car clanks past the corner of Hospital and Royal, a tremor shakes a few more crumbling grains from the arches of the old Spanish Barracks. Soon they will be returned to earth. You will forget that France gave New Orleans to Spain to pay for her help in the English wars; that

Napoleon, sitting in his bath-tub and quarreling with his brothers, maintained stoutly that since he had just forced Spain to give Louisiana back to him, he had a perfect right to re-sell; that he splashed them into agreement; and that he did re-sell the territory to the new United States. But Napoleon's legions have followed Andrew Jackson's Kentucky riflemen into the twilight.

The passing of the old order has a hundred conspicuous manifestations in New Orleans, perhaps because there is a legend for every old house, a tragedy for every shadow, a romantic blood-stain on every pavement. The Absinthe House takes in lodgers. The Cabildo, the ancient Spanish city hall, is a museum. An order of Catholic sisters now occupies the building which once witnessed the quadroon balls. There is African ragtime in New Orleans, as there is in every city and town where squeals the talking-machine, but in Beauregard Square you will not hear today the thumping of the voodoo chant, nor see the *bamboula* danced, as you might have in the days when it was Congo Square. Ashes unto ashes, dust to—reinforced concrete.

Nowhere, perhaps, is there more graphic evidence of the change than right here at Hospital and Royal Streets. Inspect the house before you. The days of its grandeur are past. The concièrge says a hundred and eighty people live there now—surely it was not intended for so many. But it is a lodging-house, and the task of cleaning up after the lodgers must make them seem to the concièrge like a hundred and eighty or more.

From the street corner diagonally opposite your eyes take in a spacious square building, three stories high, of cement-colored stucco. It has a flat roof, and its architecture suggests that the daughter of a Florentine palace became the bride of a small but snappily dressed United States Post Office. It stands flush with the *banquette*, and wears

THE HAUNTED HOUSE

a frill of balcony clear round its two street sides, under whose tempering shade you may distinguish the faded red of the lower story, and the entrance to a mysterious tunnel which is in reality a deeply arched doorway.

Under its modern exterior you will detect hints of its great age. There is, for example, a note of caprice in the red wrought-iron railings of the balcony. They may have been made, as were many in the *vieux carré*, at the very forge of Jean Lafitte, the pirate-blacksmith who commanded the marauders of Barataria, and whose pirate four-pounders helped out the rifles at the battle of New Orleans. Generations of idlers have worn smooth and rusty brown the peacock tints on the iron columns that support the balcony. There are touches of vermilion and lavender in the sharp green of the shutters at the second-floor windows.

The architecture is Italo-American, and so are the urchins popping from the doors to stare at you as you wait for admittance. Their faces are soiled, and so is the black-and-white marble floor behind the heavy spiked gates. Note, above you, the coffered and embossed ceiling, appraise the graceful fan-light over the door, examine the elaborate carving of the door itself, for these are relics which indicate the grand manner in which this house once welcomed its guests. Forget that the ceiling is blistered, that two panes are gone from the side windows, and that night-blooming lodgers have kicked the haunches off the carved steeds of Phoebus Apollo on the door. A century ago a slave would have swung wide the portal with great ceremony, and you would have mounted the winding stair to an upper hall which was notable for its elegance; today you find it dingy, uninspiring and forlorn. Not a ghost in sight anywhere.

Comes the concièrge and swears and deposes that in the year of Our Lord 1919 she did see with her own eyes a headless man march up these stairs, and that she has accordingly caused the house to be sprinkled with holy water. Did he look like Louis Philippe? Well, he looked something like him, and yet differed from him—the light wasn't good, and besides (and this *was* a happy thought) the figure had no head, and resemblances are hard to establish under those conditions. Louis Philippe is believed to have slept here, though Mr. George W. Cable doubts this, on the ground that in 1798, the year of the royal visit, no such high buildings were erected for fear they would sink into the soft ground. No, the headless man was not Louis Philippe, but some other character in the lurid history of the building.

That history began in the first year or two of the century, when the Baron de Pontalba, a stanch old Bonapartist who did as he pleased, did it with exceptionally good taste and built this mansion. Soft ground or no soft ground, the Pontalbas were a vigorous family, who, when they wanted houses, built them. Gossip said the Baron and his daughter-in-law never got on well together. There may have been some truth in it, for years later they found the Baron dead in his room at Mont l'Eveque, and daughter-in-law in her own room badly wounded by pistol shots. True, however, to the tradition of hardihood which ran in the family, she recovered, and lived through the Franco-Prussian War, carrying the bullets in her body to her grave.

The Baron had earnestly advised Napoleon to sell Louisiana to Jefferson. Oddly enough, the Purchase which he advocated brought about a change in New Orleans which attacked the very identity of such families as the Pontalbas. An invasion of uncultured Americans from the north swept down the valley, settled in the city, and beat against the social barriers of the French and Spanish circles in the *vieux carré*. Hitherto they had dictated the life of the city, and it was disturbing

THE HAUNTED HOUSE

to those who dated from the "*filles de la cassette*" and the grandees of the Spanish Main to contemplate this immigration of a new race, unancestored and, from a Latin standpoint, uncivilized. It was more than disturbing, it was electro-chemical, and although there was at first little fraternity between the races, it produced shortly a lively society.

The Duke of Saxe-Weimar is responsible for an interesting picture of its customs and habits in 1825. During a visit to New Orleans he was entertained at the home of a famous gambler, the Baron de Marigny (he who had entertained the princes of Orleans in '98), where he admired, not without cause, a set of chinaware decorated with portraits of the French royal family and its palaces. The winter was gay, and he made the rounds of dances, masques and theatres. He frequented coffee-houses, he danced with the ladies, whom he found "very pretty, with a genteel French air," and when "the gentlemen, who were far behind the ladies in elegance, did not long remain, but hastened away to other balls," he was among those also-hastening, for the naughty young gentlemen were on their way to a quadroon ball. On another occasion he called upon the august lawyer Grymes, who figured prominently in the notorious case of Salome Mueller, a white slave-girl. Grymes was a "foremost citizen" in that society, so was Miller, Salome's claimant, who probably knew she was white and therefore entitled to freedom. A foremost citizen, even in our own enlightened and prohibited day, can do no wrong—if he has the right lawyer. The Duke found the city magnificent in her unbridled emotion, charming in her graces, attractive if perverse in her ethics, and altogether capable of making a stranger's head spin.

Thus, when there came to New Orleans in 1825 a benevolent middle-aged gentleman of France, the Marquis de Lafayette, the city gave him a superlative welcome. In the light of recent Franco-American exchanges it is pleasant to think of him as the recipient of every token of hospitality the city could offer, from triumphal arches to dinners of state. It suits our specific purpose to watch him chatting in the drawing-room of the Pontalba house, to peep through the shutters of the great windows and see the street below filled with bobbing lanterns of the crowd that has collected to see the great man step into his carriage, to turn back again into the drawing-room and see that he has no intention of leaving, for he is the center of a sparkle of wit that matches the crystal chandelier for brilliance. Here he discoursed, up yonder he passed the night. With his departure in the morning, the chronicled glory of the house ends, and its tragedy begins.

Among the old court records there is an entry which establishes the fact that at the height of the interesting social period marked by Lafayette's visit the Pontalba house changed hands. On August 30, 1831, it was bought by Madame McCarty-Lopez-Blanque-Lalaurie, a woman of more than ordinary magnetism and the wife of Dr. Louis Lalaurie. Her establishment was quite up to the standards of Créole society. The touch of her expert hand was evident in the decoration of the house, and the choice and disposition of the furniture and paintings were a compliment to her taste. Her ten slaves were more than enough to care for its needs. She drove out along the Bayou road of an afternoon behind fine horses, her coachman was coveted as a correct and desirable servant. What the world calls fine people came to her house with as keen an appetite for the intellectual cocktails of the hostess as for the creature hospitality they anticipated at her table.

Like most ladies of social pursuits she had pronounced likes and dislikes, and she got herself talked about. Being a pure-blood Créole she resented the nouveau-riche American invasion of the city. "Let them come," she said. "There are some things they cannot buy"—and her good opinion was one, her invitations another. Some of "them" resented the fact that they would never be bidden to enter the deep-arched vestibule, nor see the ponderous door swing wide to them as guests, nor ascend the graceful winding stair. So they railed, and Madame Lalaurie tossed her head. They muttered unpleasant things, and she sniffed. Then they cried scandal, to which she was deaf.

A susceptible young Créole attached to the office of the district attorney was sent one day to call upon Madame Lalaurie and to bring to her attention the annoying rumor that she had been unkind to her slaves. He went away with his copy of Article XX of the Old Black Code unrecited, and his addled young head full of impatience that such slander could have been perpetrated against a person so obviously kindly as Madame Lalaurie had just shown herself to be. He had been, in fact, charmed, and he admitted it.

There is no telling how long the matter might have carried on if it had not been for a chance glimpse through a window. The unsubstantiated scandal persisted. But there happened to be a small staircase window in a neighbor's house which gave on Madame Lalaurie's courtyard, and which commanded not only the screened courtyard-galleries of the house itself but those of the slave quarters, which stood at right angles to the house.

The neighbor was going upstairs when she heard a piercing shriek. From the window she saw a little negro girl fly screaming across the courtyard, with Madame Lalaurie in close pursuit, the lady armed with a whip. Into the shelter of the house fled the child, then out again upon the lower latticed balcony. Although the neighbor could not penetrate the lattice, she followed the progress of the chase by a crescendo of terrified cries, as the child raced up the outside stairs to the next gallery, then to the next. In a moment she emerged upon the roof, her last frantic bid for sanctuary. There were seven different angles of pitch to that roof, and it was covered with shiny tiles. The child slipped, clutched, fell to the courtyard and was killed.

Madame Lalaurie buried her that night in a shallow grave in the courtyard. The neighbor saw that, too. Then, and not until then, she reported the whole episode. The authorities came and found the grave, corroborated the story, and punished Madame Lalaurie by selling all her slaves. The purchasers were her relatives, and she promptly bought all her slaves right back.

"She starves them," said Rumor, sitting on the eaves of a house across the way. "She whips them, she beats them," the story ran, gaining momentum.

"But see how fat and cheerful is her coachman," replied Reason. "Does he look like the victim of cruelty?" "He is a spy upon the others," hissed Rumor. "*Eh, bien,*" said New Orleans, and yawned lightly, "She serves such dinners!"

The slave who cooked those dinners was a radical. She tired of practising her arts with a twenty-four-foot chain clamped to her ankle. On the afternoon of April 10, 1834, after extraordinary provocation, she became desperate and set fire to the house.

The townsfolk swarmed to the fire, and were greeted at the door by the gracious Madame Lalaurie. She directed her friends in their efforts to remove her costly furniture from the house. When someone suggested seeing that there was no human life still endangered in the building she said that it was quite empty, and that there was no necessity of visiting the slave quarters. Judge Canonge took it upon himself to investigate, but the smoke drove him back. There were some in the crowd, however, who were neither her friends nor her well-

THE HAUNTED HOUSE

wishers, and who insisted that the slaves had not been removed. In the face of swelling clouds of blinding smoke and the lady's angry remonstrances, a man finally groped his way into the slave wing which stood at right angles to the house.

Within a few moments he was outside, shouting. Volunteers ran back with him into the slave quarters. In the tiny cubicles which served as living-space for those humble lives were seven negroes, some locked in while the fire crept toward them, others chained to the walls. Their emaciated bodies bore witness to famishing hunger, and cruel sores told the story of their confinement. They were carried to the street, and the crowd, having helped to put out the fire in the house, took fire itself and charged the door. Madame Lalaurie deftly slammed it in their faces.

Her resourcefulness rose to the situation. By subtle management her carriage picked its way through the crowd a few hours later and drew up at the entrance. Before the growing throng of people detected the maneuver, she and her husband were inside the equipage and rattling round the corner, "driven up Chartres Street in a close carriage which I saw speeding at a furious rate" (so Henry C. Castellanos wrote in 1895). The afternoon parade of society was idling along the Bayou Road; her skilful driver wove his way through the stream of carriages and gained fast on the pursuit which had risen, howling at her flight. The Lalauries gained the shore of Lake Pontchartrain, put off in a skiff, boarded a schooner for Mandeville—up sail, and safe away!

The coachman began his return journey to town, and ended it when he met the pack of pursuers, for they destroyed him. The chase was deferred just long enough for the lady to effect her escape to Mobile, and thence to Paris. There rumor followed, and she was avoided by society. Three years later word came back in the ships that Madame Lalaurie was dead of wounds received in a boar-hunt. She had probably hunted as hard as she had lived.

We cannot surrender her to the savage credulity of the ages, however, without suggesting that the story of her life, although generally regarded as authentic, may have been gilded here and there by intervening generations of highly-colored imagination. A New Orleans man writes:

"I happen to know one of the descendants of Madame Lalaurie very well, and I have seen a marble bust of this self-same lady whose alleged record as a slave murderer is indignantly repudiated by the self-same descendants. As a matter of fact, those stories are pretty much of a piece with those which were in vogue in regard to throwing negro slaves into the furnaces of the Mississippi River steamboats and feeding piccaninnies to alligators. This would be pretty much as if you or I stood at the foot of the Battery and chucked *all* of our money, *diamonds*, and worldly possessions into New York Bay."

That April-day crowd in New Orleans had no such sober judgment. After the coachman had been murdered they returned to Hospital and Royal Streets and sacked the house from hall to belvedere, ripped the silk curtains, slashed the paintings, tore out the chandeliers, dug up two slave skeletons from the courtyard, pitched Madame Lalaurie's precious possessions out of the windows and made bonfire of the wreckage in the street. They drank and looted and terrorized the neighborhood until a detachment of regulars appeared under the sheriff's command and put an end to the orgy.

The shell of the house stood abject and battered for a number of years, its broken windows telling its ugly story to all who came that way. On a moonlight night an impressionable girl passing the house could readily have seen the ghost of a woman's form leaning imploringly

THE HAUNTED HOUSE

from the belvedere—one girl did see it, and not even her later confession that the ghost was a fabric of moonbeams has been sufficient to rid the building of its name—The Haunted House. Nor, when inside the stout old walls a new and finer residence was built in cheerful defiance of the ghost, could the spirit of tragedy be easily banished. We shall hear one more story—a brief one—and then we may judge.

The war came and passed and left New Orleans dominated politically by those who had been their slaves. The pendulum swung so far to the extreme that a public school for both white and black children was ordained and, by coincidence or cunning design, was established in the Haunted House. It was of course an unfortunate move, and served no purpose except to whet racial antagonism. There came, finally, the breaking point. A white political organization which had been recuperating in strength sent a delegation one afternoon to call at the school. They were met by the teachers, to whom they issued a command to muster the school for roll-call. One of the pupils, a girl of exceptional beauty, heard the commotion from the upper hall, and peering over the banisters realized the significance of the roll-call—that the white pupils were to be segregated from the black. She leaned far over, to catch every word, when a shell comb fell from her hair and shattered on the marble floor below. She burst into tears and fled to an upper room.

The roll-call ended. All pupils who had negro blood were ordered from the house. When the slight flurry had subsided, and the delegation had left, the principal and one of the teachers found Marguerite upstairs in a paroxysm of grief. "The comb was my mother's," she sobbed, and when the teacher tried to comfort her, became hysterical. The principal drew the teacher outside. "It is not on account of the comb," she said. "Marguerite's mother was an octoroon; she married a white sea-captain. He loved her so much that in order to marry her he opened his wrist and let a few drops of her blood into his own, so that he might swear that he had African blood in his veins and get a marriage license. Only Marguerite and I and one or two others knew her story—and no one would have suspected, for she is so beautiful. She is engaged to be married, and her fiancé didn't know. But the roll-call—now she will leave school, and he must learn of it."

Which was the greater tragedy—the brutality of slave torture, or the death of the exquisite school-girl's romance? It may be you will find the answer from the ghost, if ten years of children's lessons, and the arpeggios and trills of a conservatory of music, and subsequent vapors of lodging-house cooking have not frightened the ghost herself away. Go and see. Far and down in the old quarter of New Orleans, where Hospital Street meets Royal, you will scarcely hear the drone of the modern city at work. In the *vieux carré* one may converse easily with ghosts. You will find no answer here.

Doughoregan Manor

DOUGHOREGAN MANOR

There are three ghosts at Doughoregan Manor. One is the shade of an ancient housekeeper, whose quiet tread may be heard in the corridors, and whose keys tinkle faintly when the house is still. Another is the spectral coach—its wheels grind on the driveway when death rides to claim a member of the household. . . . The third is no gruesome phantom, but the warm lively pervading spirit of the Signer himself, Charles Carroll "*of Carrollton.*"

Doughoregan Manor

YOU may come up a long straight aisle of locust trees, or you may wind through Gothic arches of elms along a skilfully engineered road which picks its way through the estate for a half-mile or more. Either course will bring you before a wide low house of yellow brick, with green blinds and white woodwork and English ivy. Directly ahead of you, across the circle of the driveway, the square main section of the house, capped by a tower, rises above a bright portico. To left and right the house throws out long extensions of even height, terminating in wings set endwise to you, like double-faces in the game of dominoes. Your first impression will be one of unusual size, your next of flatly rectangular simplicity. Your eye will be caught momentarily by a cross-tipped bell-tower of the right wing, where Charles Carroll built the only private chapel in America because England would not let him worship in peace. You will know that you have never seen such a house in America, and you will probably not suspect that it is a monument to several great Americans.

A lad of four or five is playing on the grass circle of the driveway before the great house. The undulating Maryland countryside is not half as absorbing as the game in hand, though his great-grandfather was governor of all those miles. If you were to ask him the way to Annapolis he would probably indicate the double file of venerable trees which stand sentinel along the tapering avenue, smile courteously if you thanked him, and then scurry off on an important engagement. He wouldn't tell you that in his grandfather's great-grandfather's day Annapolis was the national capital, nor that that gentleman was one of the bold spirits who made a national capital possible.

There is no reason why he should know of it, or be interested. If, with your heavy wisdom, and your rhapsodies on the pride of race, and your generally affable tourist behavior you succeed in alarming the lad until he retreats to the shelter of the portico, know, stranger, that you have aroused the suspicions of Charles Carroll, the Ninth in America, and the seventh heir of that name to Doughoregan Manor.

Ancestors can be lived up to or lived down, and there is no particular point or prowess in bragging about them. To me there is glorious romance in the fact that this youngster of five is romping on the ground that was granted to his ancestor by a King of England. Perhaps it is glorious and romantic because it is fact, but I prefer to believe that the real reason may be found in a verse in the book of Exodus, which reads:

"Honor thy father and thy mother."

They were worth honoring; they have been duly honored even unto the eighth and ninth generations.

Charles Carroll the First, like many another Irishman since, went west. He came to Baltimore in 1688 with the ink hardly sanded on his commission as attorney-general of Maryland. As a Roman Catholic he found the commission suddenly nullified by revolution in England, and it was four years before a Royal government was set up in the colony restoring and protecting its proprietary rights. His wife had died childless during that period, and he married again. Of ten children of his second wife, the eldest died on the voyage home from school in Europe. Back at St. Omer's in French Flanders he left a younger brother, Charles Carroll the Second, and presently the plodding ships bore back to him the news of Henry's death and the heritage of responsibility and affection which devolved upon him. In 1723 he came back to his own people, married in his turn, and in 1737 Mistress Elizabeth Brooke Carroll bore him a son. The precedent for the name Charles was already strong, Charles was a good name, and so was christened Charles Carroll the Third.

In the archives of the State Department at Washington you will find his signature. It is hidden from the light, but reproductions of it and the pledge to which it is attached have already made it familiar to every American. The story runs that in the congress at Philadelphia when the Declaration of Independence was presented, John Hancock turned to Carroll and offering him a quill, asked "Will you sign?"

"Most willingly," was the reply. And he signed, in an easy clear hand, with less flourish, perhaps, than Franklin's or Hancock's, but no less sincerity—and Carroll, the richest man in America, had more to lose than either.

"There goes two millions with the dash of a pen!" a bystander remarked. "Oh, Carroll, you will get off," said another. "There are so many Charles Carrolls." At which Charles Carroll Third took the pen and jabbed "of Carrollton" under his signature, that George Third of England might make no mistake and punish any other of the same name. There is some cherry-tree flavor in the story, and precious historians maintain that he invariably signed his full title; but, if it can accomplish by example what the cherry-tree fable has accomplished, let it stand.

What circumstances carried this patriot, whom we left a moment ago as a baby, to the front rank of his country's champions? The best of schooling then was to be had abroad. An ardent father and mother put aside their fierce attachment to their only child in order that he might become a proper heir to the estate which Charles Carroll the Second was accumulating. Just as the young Pinckneys and Rutledges and Middletons of Charleston in pre-Revolutionary days went to the mother country for their cultural training, so the youths of the middle states whose families could afford the excursion were dispatched to France, or England, or Flanders. One day in 1748 saw Charles Carroll, a boy of eleven, take ship with his cousin John for Europe. What pangs his mother experienced at the loss of her only chick are faintly reflected in a passage from the correspondence between the two: "You are always at heart my dear Charley and I have never tired of asking your papa questions about you. I daily pray to God to grant you his grace above all things, and to take you under his protection." "With your mother," his father wrote in 1753, "I shall be glad to have your likeness in the compass of 15 inches by 12"—and directed him to have the specified portrait done by a good painter. But the mother was not well, and in 1761, when the baby who had sailed away was a grown man, a student of Law in the Temple in London, and nearly ready to return to the warmth of his mother's adoration, she died.

Such a beau as he would have made her! Heredity gave him an active mind and bearing of real charm, and just as the Manor house back in Maryland took on through the years extensions and embellishments which multiply its effect of useful luxury, so each addition to Charles Carroll's intellect only seemed to make him more companionable and genuinely attractive. Even during his student period his sensitive spirit was not altogether proof against affairs of the heart, and if it had not been for her meddlesome sister, Miss Louisa Baker would have gone back to Maryland as his bride, as mistress over 68,000 acres. Instead, the catch of the commonwealth returned at twenty-nine under a cloak of melancholy from the shelter of which he wrote, dourly, "Matrimony is at present but little the subject of my thoughts."

Persons familiar with the laws of gravity and more particularly with the physics of the rebounding heart will not be surprised to learn that within a few months he was again engaged to be married, this time to Miss Rachel Cooke. He wrote to London for her trousseau—such intimate finery as he hardly dared describe, things to turn even the Babylonian fiancée of today as green with envy as the Doughoregan meadows. But the Brussels lace was not for her, for Rachel Cooke fell ill of a fever, and died, and her miniature and a lock of her tresses were hidden away in a secret partition of Charles Carroll's writing desk.

Undiscouraged, he found serious distraction in the fermenting affairs of the colonies. From provincial grievances such as his father had related from time to time in his letters dwelling on the oppression of the rights of Catholics, the problems of the colonists had overflowed greater areas. Like a flood swelling over the landscape, the minor swirls of flow and eddy were merged into a common misfortune of drab color and threatening proportions. It was Charles Carroll's first chance for constructive citizenship. At the writing-desk where Rachel's miniature lay hidden he wrote a program of letters which may be said to constitute the brief for independence. And by the time his heart had healed, and he had fallen in love with Miss Mary Darnell, whom he preferred, he said, "to all the women I have ever seen, even to Louisa," and had married her, he was caught in the flood himself. There was no turning back even if he wanted to—and he did not want to turn back.

His town house at Annapolis and the manor of Doughoregan (it is pronounced *Dooráygan*, and it means the house of the king, because a thousand years or so ago the O'Carrolls were Irish kings) opened their doors with special welcome to those who were prepared to resist the oppression of a king. "A warm, firm, zealous supporter of the rights of America, in whose cause he has hazarded his all," wrote John Adams, Carroll's "all" at that time yielding an income of some ten thousand pounds a year. When, in 1773, an outraged importer set fire to his cargo of taxed tea in Annapolis, Charles Carroll was his chief legal counsel. When the Continental Congress met in Philadelphia the next year, he was a member. When the Congress sent a delegation to Canada to enlist support for the Revolution, it seized upon his French training as an asset in Charles Carroll, as it chose Benjamin Franklin for his practical judgment, Father John Carroll (later the first Archbishop of Baltimore) for his ecclesiastical influence, and Samuel Chase for his legal ability. The mission failed; Canada would not help; we must work alone. So to indicate that he welcomed the opportunity Charles Carroll signed the Declaration of Independence.

Years later he wrote this summary of his career:

"On the breaking out of the Revolution I took a decided part in the support of the rights of this country; was elected a member of the Committee of Safety established by the Legislature; was a member of the Convention which formed the Constitution of the State. The Journals of Congress show how long I was a member of that body during the Revolution. With Dr. Franklin and Mr. Samuel Chase I was appointed a Commissioner to Canada. I was elected a member of the Senate at the first session of Congress under the present Confederation. . . . The mode of choosing the Senate was suggested by me. . . ."

That was all he found to write. It ought to be enough to qualify him for the emphasis which, in the eminent line of Charles Carrolls, we have placed upon him. But if, after you have followed him through the Revolution, you inquire just what connection the details of his career have with Doughoregan Manor, listen to a short recital of what he was too modest to write.

In 1780 his father, Charles the Second, was standing on the veranda of his Annapolis house and peering through a spy-glass at a sail in the Bay. He made a misstep, pitched heavily from the porch, and was killed. Mary Darnell Carroll, his daughter-in-law, saw him fall. Her health, already taxed by her devotion to Mrs. Carroll II during her last illness, gave way at "Breakneck" Carroll's tragic death, and she died within a fortnight, leaving to her husband a son and two daughters. The son, of course, was Charles Carroll the Fourth. The Signer saw him go to Liége to school, return, as his father had returned before him, the idol of a gay countryside, court Nellie Custis at Mount Vernon, marry Harriet Chew of Cliveden, and rejoice with pride at the advent in 1801 of Charles Carroll the Fifth.

Charles the Fourth, of Homewood, has been described by a contemporary as follows: "Nothing in Greek art surpasses the perfect symmetry of his figure." No less a person than Washington had asked Harriet Chew to remain in his presence while he sat for his portrait to Gilbert Stuart in order that his own face might "wear its most agreeable expression." Therefore if the baby Charles the Fifth was not handsome it was neither the fault of his parents nor of the distinguished grandfather who immediately became his devoted slave.

The concerns of the estate, and the larger questions of the nation, had the Signer's first attention. His avocations were to ride his lanes and woodland, to read Greek and Latin in the original—he was reading Cicero's "De Senectute" at ninety-three; to preside over a growing flock of grandchildren at Homewood with his son, at Brooklandwood, where Mary Carroll Caton was bringing up the three stunning daughters whom society called the "American Graces"; and to spend much time in the company of his daughter Kitty's husband, Robert Goodloe Harper. From time to time he was called upon to step into his earlier character as Signer. In 1824 he was invited, with Jefferson and Madison, the only survivors of that great company who fixed their names to the Declaration, to attend the anniversary of the surrender of Cornwallis at Yorktown. His age forced him to decline, but he compromised by meeting Lafayette at Fort McHenry and lunching with him in a tent which had been Washington's, and by attending a ball given in Lafayette's honor at Colonel Howard's "Belvedere."

Few men of eighty-seven have shown such activity as was his; most men of his years would have given way to the misfortunes which now trooped out of the shadows. Charles Carroll the Fourth died; General Harper, the beloved son-in-law, followed. In the next year John Adams and Thomas Jefferson died on the same day, and it was the sad duty of Charles the Third to mourn at their funeral. He was now the last of the Signers. At eighty-nine he signed a copy of the Declaration which is now held in the New York Public Library—and signed it in a handwriting as firm as it had been fifty years before; at ninety he laid the foundation stone of the Baltimore & Ohio Railroad; at ninety-three the cornerstone of St. Charles' College, near Doughoregan Manor. And by this time the patriarch had seen born into his grandson's family a sixth Charles Carroll.

There are three ghosts at Doughoregan Manor. One is the shade of an ancient housekeeper, whose quiet tread may be heard in the corridors, and whose keys tinkle faintly when the house is still. Another is the spectral coach—its wheels grind on the driveway when death rides to claim a member of the household—the coach which swung up to the door on a still November day in 1832 when the Signer went to join his fathers. It is hardly dignified to call the third a ghost. A warm, lively, pervading spirit it is—that of the Signer himself, smiling down from his portrait on the walls. It beamed on Charles the Sixth through a long and active life until it beckoned to him in 1895. To the son of Charles Carroll VI, John Lee Carroll, it nodded: "Well done, my boy," when he became Governor of Maryland, and to the seventh Charles it told again all that its cumulative history could convey of the philosophical guidance and binding parental attachment that has made Doughoregan Manor something more than a home. Charles Bancroft Carroll, the Eighth, "carries on" and injects typical enthusiasm into farming twenty-four hundred acres of the grant you will see in the hall on a map the first Charles Carroll drew.

You will feel the spirit strongly as you contemplate the Signer's place of burial in the chapel where the countryside gathers each Sunday for services. You will sense the alliance between devotion to God and to profoundly national ideals, and recall the sympathetic correspondence between the Signer and his father, as you enter the Cardinal's room, a gorgeous chamber decorated in red, containing a great mahogany bed where Cardinal Gibbons, Archbishop John Carroll, and the Marquis de Lafayette have slept. In a mellow library are the books he read. Trophies over the door of a panelled dining-room, cups won at yachting, a friendly hound from the present master's hunting pack at your feet—remember that the Signer believed that a clear mind was most likely to be found in a sound body. We may fairly conceive that when the house was to be renovated, as it has been four times in its history, the Signer laid a gentle hand upon the sleeve of the workmen and cautioned them so: "Paint, if you like. Replace, where the old has given all its service. But remember, sirs, this is and must be a home." And in the fullest connotation of the word, it is a home, with old chairs to fit you, bright cretonnes at the windows, and friendly things about you to rest your eyes upon—the sort of a home that a lad like Charles Carroll the Ninth, who isn't much interested in ancestors, likes to take refuge in when strangers grow inquisitive.

THE JUMEL MANSION

THE JUMEL MANSION

Alone in its brittle modern neighborhood, this lovely anachronism stands on the highest point of Manhattan, untroubled, unruffled, and undisturbed except by Sunday idlers to whom its orchards are just another breathing spot. Though it was Heath's headquarters, then housed Washington, later was captured by Howe, and was one of the smartest suburban estates of Colonial New York, it will never be forgotten as the home of a person of no military or aristocratic consequence, yet of caprice, beauty, ambition, impropriety, common sense and eccentricity—yes, a woman.

THE JUMEL MANSION

A LITTLE over a hundred years have passed. Much sea-water has pressed up the Harlem on the incoming tide, boiled and eddied in the narrow pass of Spuyten Duyvil, and slipped away again to the Atlantic, diluted by the contribution of mountain streams in the Catskills and Adirondacks, tainted by the factory waste of busy cities up the Hudson and the Mohawk. Men threw giant bridges across its ebb and flow, tunneled under its current, bit and blasted and scratched at its Hell Gate channel. The placid, austere heights that stood above the stream "nine miles from New York City" bear now the unromantic name of Coogan's Bluff, and are as many miles within the city's northern limits.

The camera had not been invented when Roger Morris built the house for his young wife. To the westward, where his acreage touched the Hudson, apartment houses have risen and cut off the Palisades; to the south, where once he could see far down Staten Island, a tangle of bridges and shipping is half screened by the battlements of more apartment buildings; only to the east and north, over the sunny throat of the Sound and the far blue profile of the Long Island hills, has the prospect its former grand, pure simplicity. A fan of railway tracks are at the Harlem where once was "Fishing, Oystering and Clamming," and from the very skirts of the estate rises each afternoon the roar of fifteen or twenty thousand "busy Americans" who are totally unoccupied except with the baseball game in process on the Polo Grounds.

FAMOUS COLONIAL HOUSES

It is hard, without photographic record, to reconstruct the picture. Alone in its brittle modern neighborhood this lovely anachronism is the only fragment of the composition left to us. It stands on the highest point of York Island, untroubled, unruffled, and for the most part undisturbed, except by Sunday idlers to whom its orchards are just another breathing spot.

It may be unjust to the Jumel Mansion to compare it with the lady in one of Leonard Merrick's stories who "had outgrown her sins, but remembered them with pleasure," but the spirit of Madame Jumel haunts the air so persistently that the suggestion is not altogether out of place. Despite the fact that when the British were advancing across Long Island in 1776 it was General Heath's headquarters, that it housed Washington for six weeks, and that fifteen minutes after he had left it on the day Fort Washington was taken General Howe established his own headquarters there—despite its standing as one of the smartest suburban estates of Colonial New York, the house will never be forgotten as the home of a person of no military or aristocratic consequence, yet a person of caprice and beauty, ambition and impropriety, common sense and eccentricity. She was no sort of person to talk about, and therefore talked about; a kaleidoscopic contradiction—in short, a woman.

Though General Washington probably never heard of the lady, the house which she occupied was strangely related to important moments in his own career. When he was an athletic officer of twenty-five, neither Betsy Bowen nor her mother, Phebe Kelly of Providence, knew of him or cared about him, for they were both yet unborn. Of his restrained sentimental interest for Polly Philipse, the Yonkers heiress, they could not know, nor had they comment to offer when Colonel Roger Morris, a gallant of the colonial forces, crowded

THE JUMEL MANSION

the young Virginian out of her affections and married her. In 1760 when Washington himself married Martha Custis, Phebe Kelly was three years old; at the age of eighteen, in the same month when Washington was appointed commander-in-chief of the American army and rode to its head at Cambridge, Phebe Kelly Bowen of Providence gave birth to her second daughter, and called her Betsy.

Ten years before, Roger Morris had built a lovely house for his wife and their growing family on the topmost point of Manhattan; the wailing baby in Providence in that turbulent July, 1775, scarcely suspected that one day she would be the mistress of that house, or that a month ago Roger Morris, a Tory, too peaceful to fight, had fled to England for refuge. But there began the chain of events which finally landed his estate in Betsy Bowen's hands.

The city of Providence was so named because its founders had supreme confidence in its namesake. With the advent of a pathetic little atom of humanity called Betsy Bowen, Providence the power, through the agency of Providence the city, undertook to show off. "Her father was a seafaring man of no account; her mother of less," said the town. "It looks bad. It probably is. If not, it ought to be. In any case, Providence shall be appeased." Betsy's mother was presently arrested and thrown in jail, and Betsy, with her sister Polly, then a child of fourteen, was first locked up in the workhouse and later sent to live with a more respectable family. John Bowen, the father, was knocked overboard by the boom of a sloop and drowned; his widow and her second husband were allowed out of jail long enough to be ordered out of town; they returned and were shortly expelled at the expense of the town, to carry on a wretched existence in a hut on the Old Warren Road. As the daughters matured they moved to a less respectable family. In 1794 a son was born to Betsy Bowen, and its father's name being either unknown, undesirable or Jones, the baby was christened George Washington Bowen. Three years later her mother and her step-father, once more expelled from Providence, made their way to the North Carolina mountains, got sufficiently acquainted with their neighbors to start a lawsuit, and then were shot by a squirrel rifle in the hands of one or more of the defendants. Providence the town had forgotten them, Providence the power had accomplished a *tour de force.*

The divine lightnings were apparently spent. Betsy Bowen left her baby in the hands of a friend and fled from the mockery of her native city. She began six obscure years of adventure as Betsy Bowen, reappeared in New York for a fleeting glimpse as Madame De la Croix, and emerged as Eliza Brown, the mistress of the wealthy Stephen Jumel. From 1800 to 1804 she occupied this prosperous French merchant's house at the corner of Whitehall and Pearl Streets, near the lower tip of Manhattan. He came home one day to find her apparently on her death bed, explaining faintly, through the medium of her physician, that she wanted nothing more than to leave a sorry world as his wife. To Jumel, who was deeply touched, it was an irresistible appeal, and the clergyman who had come to pray for her married the pair. No hypodermic has since been discovered by a vaulting medical science which ever had such magical powers of restoration, for two days later Betsy Bowen-de la Croix-Brown-Jumel was riding out behind Stephen Jumel's smart horses as Stephen Jumel's lawful, gleeful, wedded wife. Her program, after a bad start, was fairly begun.

She craved social prominence. She wanted to hob-nob with such folk as the Philipses, the rich Astors, the Van Cortlandts, the Lows, and the Livingstons, none of whom would have much to do with her. The leverage of owning one of the great estates evidently did not occur

THE JUMEL MANSION

to her just yet, though there was one to be had. In a letter from Aaron Burr to his daughter Theodosia, then married and living in the Pringle house in Charleston, he wrote: "Roger Morris's place, the large handsome house on the height beyond Mrs. Watkins, is for sale. I can get it for Richmond Hill with *four* acres. Shall I exchange? R. M.'s has one hundred and thirty acres. If I leave Richmond Hill, however, had I not better buy in town, that you may have a resting place here?"

He evidently rejected the idea. He could not foresee that within a few months he would retire from the vice-presidency of the United States, bully Alexander Hamilton into a duel on the Palisades, kill him; nor that he would then organize an invasion of Mexico and a revolution in the new Louisiana Purchase only to be caught in the act and be tried for treason; nor that the year 1810 would find him abroad, disgraced, and still plotting to capture Mexico.

In that year Stephen Jumel, who had taken his wife's trick-marriage in good part, bought the Roger Morris house and transferred his family to the heights, to install his wife in a style of living to which she hoped to become accustomed. Nothing was nearer her heart than the social prestige which her position as the chatelaine of a fine estate would afford, nothing farther from her mind than a lonesome ex-vice-president who had once speculated on buying this very house. The God of Coincidence made a mental note of this, and laid his plans.

Although frequent changes of ownership and lack of care had tarnished the house, it was intrinsically the same fine honest mansion that Roger Morris built, with two-foot outer walls lined with English brick, and supporting timbers of enduring oak. Madame Jumel entered her new home through a lofty portico to a main hall which runs through the center of the building from front to rear. This hall leads, as at Monticello, to an octagonal annex which is the only departure from a rather simple Georgian plan. To her left a reception room, to her right the dining-room, ahead in the octagon, a drawing-room which commanded nearly the full circle of that far-reaching panorama. Here had been held the Revolutionary courts-martial. The room north of the reception room had been the commander-in-chief's office; the southeast bedroom had been his, and from its window he could see the smoking embers of the fire set by his troops when they evacuated the city in '76—the night Nathan Hale was caught there as a spy.

With Roger Morris a fugitive in London and the house in debatable ground, Polly Philipse Morris had resorted to the Manor at Yonkers for safety. When Washington was driven out, and the house became British headquarters, the army paid rent, but when the Revolution ended, the families of Morris and Philipse, their properties confiscated, went back to England. The mansion was sold and resold, but no one held it for long. It failed as a tavern, and was doubtless expensive to run as a home.

Jumel was a great admirer of Washington, as well as a man of taste, and he combined the two qualities to restore the house implicitly to its earlier condition. It meant a lot to him that Washington, the president, had dined a brilliant company there in 1790, when New York was the national capital, and he equipped the room with fine furniture brought from France in one of his packets. He had the wallpaper in the octagon copied and rehung, respected the simplicity of the mantels, and chose his decorative "remarks" with a nice eye. When his work was done we may fancy that he rubbed his hands and said to his pretty wife: "*Voilà!* A house worthy of its guests. Let them come, my dear."

They didn't come. Everything domestic a woman could crave Betsy Jumel had, even the company of her step-sister's little daughter, to take the part of the daughter she never had. It was not enough. Five years of it made her despise the place. So the Jumels packed up and sailed for France.

It was no expeditionary force against a new stronghold of society, but an innocent visit to relatives, and perhaps that is why her luck turned. Family tradition has it that in Bordeaux they met the fleeing Napoleon, and offered him the Jumel ship. In return he gave them his carriage, for which he had no further use, and they drove in it to Paris.

Such credentials opened every door of the Bonapartist royalty. Everything Madame Jumel would have wished to be in New York she became in Paris—a turn of fortune which has come to many a socially ambitious American woman since. New avenues of association opened, and she tried to cajole Louis XVIII into giving Stephen a title. What Stephen would have liked better was money for two ships the French government stole from him, for the demands of his expensive establishment in the Place Vendome and a few strokes of ill luck in trading were reducing his funds. When his position grew embarrassing his wife left him and returned to New York.

Two years later—in 1828—Stephen Jumel followed her. Dark rumor says that it was very late when he drove out from town, and that as he approached the mansion he passed Aaron Burr, who was leaving it. He entered, and found that his wife, with the expert legal assistance of Alexander Hamilton, Jr., had transferred the propery from her name to his. Four years later he fell from a hay-cart, and in a few days died of his injuries, and whoever took the bandage off those injuries and let him bleed to death will answer for that crime elsewhere, for it is not known in this world.

On a midsummer night of 1833, presided over by the God of

Coincidence, Aaron Burr came to the mansion to play whist with the widow. "Madame," he said, "I offer you my hand; my heart has long been yours." If you will believe her own version of this proposal from a veteran of seventy-eight, she made no reply. He came the next night, with a priest. She fled upstairs. He overtook her at the landing, "saying the priest was old, and it was nearly midnight, and I must not detain him—and he was so handsome and brave and I allowed him to keep my hand and I stood up there . . . and like a fool was married to him! The wretch, but he did not stay here long."

A few days he stayed, and left her, after a wedding trip in the course of which she sold some stock in Hartford and scornfully bade the purchaser "pay the money to my husband." Months later he was persuaded to rejoin her, but it could not last. A divorce ensued, and Aaron Burr died.

There really ends the career of Madame Jumel. But she lived through the Mexican and the Civil wars. Here and there in the city, now at Saratoga, once in Europe, she "lived around" with relatives of sorts, but most of the time she spent in the great house. Its corners grew less and less neat as age crept over her. Still, however, the active physique her sea-faring father and her tomboy mother had given little Betsy Bowen held on grimly to life and activity, and the social mania which had consumed her thoughts lighted up her memory with fantasies, as a sputtering lantern creates half-authentic figures among the shadows of a dusty, neglected stage. Outside the house she had no friends except those who wanted her money or stole her firewood and livestock, indoors life was a perpetual pageant. For twenty years a feast table, fully set, with dust in the crystal wine glasses, and mould on the petrifying candies, stood in a closed room: this, she related, was the table at which she had entertained Joseph Bonaparte when he came over to marry her and her riches and had to climb over the back wall to gain entrance. She took pity on him then, she said, for it didn't look just right to have the King of Spain in the kitchen. The truth is that she never entertained Joseph Bonaparte (though she offered him the estate in 1820); nor did the Duke of Palermo offer to marry the "Vice-Queen of America" as she styled herself (although she inspected the ducal palace in Palermo); she was in Paris when Lafayette visited America in 1825, but she honestly believed that she had been his hostess on the Heights. Some recollection of a name, a face, a romantic anecdote out of her vivid past popped up, or she ran across one of the dingy, pathetic dance favors or trinkets or ribbons of a dead affair, and presto!—her feverish mind whirled away in a jumbled drama, unlimited in its romantic action, and delicious in its inaccuracy.

If the public saw her it was under circumstances that magnified all the erratic tales that were—and still are—current about her history. One winter she took a group of penniless Frenchmen under her wing, quartered them in the barn, which had once held American prisoners, armed them from the arsenal she kept in the house, organized them into a military outfit, and would ride proudly at their head over her estate. From France she brought home green livery for her postilions —though she had no postilions, and when taunting reached her ears she dressed the gardener and his boy in the livery and rode to town with them. Her face to the world was as haughty and as tinctured with rouge as if she were Eliza Brown of Whitehall Street, her dress as shabby-genteel as she fancied it was fashionable, her intellect as tragically aflame with the mad dance of Might-Have-Been as it was fixed, cold, and shrewd in financial matters. *Grande dame* she had set out to be, *grande dame* she had become, and mercifully to the poor little shrunken creature with the powdered cheeks and the soiled finery who was finally carried upstairs to the Washington room to die, *grande dame* in her mind she died.

It was a signal for the jackals. No less than twenty law-suits sprang up to break the will and seize the property. Some of the claims seem just, others less so, and all of them, in the course of fifty years, have gone through the mill of the courts and been ground exceeding fine. Of them all, the most interesting fragment is the attempt made by George Washington Bowen, Betsy's deserted baby in Providence, to own his mother's home. For thirteen years the old man pursued his case, even to the Supreme Court, lost it, and died, though the claim is still cherished by his own connections. The estate could not hold out long against the march of the city, and parcel by parcel it was split up, until in 1894 the house and its dooryard came into the hands of General F. P. Earle.

The city owns it now, and four capable chapters of the Daughters of the American Revolution have formed the Washington Headquarters Association, and have brought the mansion out of neglect and oblivion. They opened the windows Madame Jumel kept sealed and let in air and sunlight; they consigned the Eastlake-and-gimcrack whatnottery of its most recent tenants to the exceedingly efficent ash-removal department of the City of New York, which is equipped to handle just such situations, and from the four corners of our country they assembled and installed in the house as much of its historic equipment as they could find. There is much of it, of course, which has no special significance, and there is so great a quantity of relics there that the house is in no sense a home, but rather an interesting and valuable museum. Next best of all, they opened the doors to the public in a city where sorely-needed Americanization may well begin at home. And best of all, they installed as curator William Henry Shelton, as

THE JUMEL MANSION

gracious a story-teller as the humble history-seeker may ply with questions. It is to him largely that the excellent administration of the house is due. It is he who can bid you close your eyes, make a few passes, and translate you into the presence of Mary Philipse, or bring you to attention before George Washington, or open a secret panel that you may peep at Madame Jumel. In his book, "The Jumel Mansion," he has done just this, and it is from that source with his permission that the greater part of this story is drawn, and so, gratefully acknowledged.

MOUNT VERNON

MOUNT VERNON

Here on a hill in Fairfax County, Virginia, we may catch glimpses of the man George Washington liked to be.

MOUNT VERNON

THE First President once wrote a letter to a Charleston gentleman named Thomas Pinckney, who was then American ambassador at the British court. His words were for Thomas Pinckney, not for posterity, so posterity finds it refreshing to see a president writing a specific letter to his envoy under the pitiless light of publicity. Its chief interest here is not his report of the Senate's action on a proposed treaty with Great Britain, nor his anxiety over Lafayette's imprisonment in Olmutz, though both are subjects upon which he dwells at some length. The note for us is the fact that after long diplomatic instruction to his ambassador, Washington says:

"Before I close this letter permit me to request the favour of you to embrace some favorable opportunity to thank Lord Grenville in my behalf, for his politeness in causing a special permit to be sent to Liverpool for the shipment of two sacks of the field peas, and the like quantity of winter vetches, which I had requested our Consul at that place to send me for seed, but which it seems cannot be done without a special order from Government. A circumstance which did not occur to me, or I certainly should not have given it the trouble of issuing one for such a trifle.

"With very great esteem and regard
"I am, dear Sir,
"Your obedt. Servant,
"G. Washington."

FAMOUS COLONIAL HOUSES

A treaty with Great Britain, Lafayette to be got out of prison, two sacks of field peas and some winter vetch—and there is George Washington. Our national heroes march down the ages without time to change costumes. While they live we call them everything under the sun; they die, and we endow them with a certain type-quality which they must wear forever to the exclusion of other and equally interesting qualities which they possessed in equal quantity. Unless some circumstance rescue those qualities from oblivion, a large part of the inspiration of their lives has been unnecessarily sacrificed. We have seen the first manifestation of such a process with the death of Colonel Roosevelt, and we wonder how frequently our children's children will think of Roosevelt on the tennis-court, at Sagamore, in Montana, in Rock Creek Park, or facing death in Brazil. The nation loses a man, to mourn a saint. So in a lesser degree with our lesser heroes: Hale becomes the lay-figure of Loyalty, Franklin, of Common Sense, Grant, of Military Patience. Here, on a hill in Fairfax County, Virginia, in and about a great white house, we may catch glimpses of the man George Washington liked to be—glimpses denied us in the popular Washington legend.

He was a boy of three when his father first brought him there. He was seven when his father's house burned, and the discouragement and loneliness of the wilderness plantation on the Potomac sent the young family to Fredericksburg to live. He was fifteen when he came back to live on the Potomac estate, now the property of his brother Lawrence. Lawrence was of no mean importance in his young brother's eye—a veteran of the West Indian naval exploits of Admiral Vernon, and so full of them that he named the estate after his chief—altogether a rare big brother. And there were rare neighbors to be cultivated: like Lord Fairfax, an Oxford graduate and contributor to Mr.

Addison's *Spectator*, who took a fellow riding, and now and then rode after a fox.

As the boy broadened into self-reliance in such company as Lawrence's, and into a degree of education by association with Fairfax, he fell heir to certain of their responsibilities. Fairfax sent him to survey his vast holdings. Lawrence developed tuberculosis, and his military duties devolved upon George. At twenty he was master of Mount Vernon, at twenty-one a lieutenant-colonel and fighting for the English against the French on the Ohio. Thackeray has pointed, in this episode, the caprice of fate: "It was strange that in a savage forest of Pennsylvania a young Virginian officer should fire a shot and waken up a war which was to last for sixty years, which was to cover his own country and pass into Europe, to cost France her American colonies, to sever ours from us, and create the great Western Republic; to rage over the Old World when extinguished in the New; and, of all the myriads engaged in the vast contest, to leave the prize of the greatest fame with him who struck the first blow!"

The next year he was a part of Braddock's disastrous expedition, and news went home that he had been killed. John Augustine Washington made alarmed inquiries, to which George replied with a wit equal to Mark Twain's under similar circumstances: "As I have heard, since my arrival at this place, a circumstantial account of my death and dying speech, I take this early opportunity of contradicting the first, and of assuring you that I have not as yet composed the latter." He became a member of the legislature, and then, when he was twenty-six and a full colonel, he married Martha Dandridge Custis, who was by all odds the most accomplished and probably the wealthiest young widow in Williamsburg. It was time now to renew his neglected acquaintance with Mount Vernon.

During the period of their engagement, while Washington was absent at the frontier, and later, while he was attending the session of the House of Burgesses at Williamsburg, Mount Vernon, which had been so long neglected, was taking on a new dress. The activity on the plantation was contagious. It spread down river, to Belvoir, to Gunston Hall, and through the countryside to the other estates where Washington was intimately known, and where his earlier and generous attentions to attractive daughters did nothing to dampen their interest in his bride. Their swift coach-ride homeward bound from Williamsburg was like a triumphal entry. She added to his holdings of twenty-five hundred acres at Mount Vernon, and as many over the mountains, some fifteen thousand acres of her own. She found the house rebuilt, its exterior strengthened by new brick burned on the estate, new boarding and sheathing, new windows and a new roof; inside was new plaster, new flooring, and plenty of new closet-room, which probably touched her woman's heart as inexpressibly thoughtful.

"I am now I believe fixd at this seat with an agreeable Consort for Life," he wrote to a friend in England. "And I hope to find more happiness in retirement than I ever experienced amidst a wide and bustling World." Few realize how wide and bustling was the world surveyed from Mount Vernon, nor to what extent he exerted himself to make use of the talents he had been given. Remember that there were no neighboring shops, no groceries, no service stations—not one, in fact, of the multitude of helping hands which science reaches out today to perform every conceivable task; and remember too that in his custody were, and upon his wise management depended, not only the happiness of his wife and her two children, but that of a company of several hundred others on the estate.

Husband and wife shared in an informal copartnership not unlike that of a manufacturer and a retail store-manager of today. It was her duty to anticipate the living demands of the estate, his to supply them. When she requisitioned cloth, he built a spinning-house and hired labor which in one year spun fourteen hundred yards of textiles, from broadcloth to bed-ticking. Convenient to the house, and flanking the serpentine drive, were his little factories: a smokehouse for meats, a laundry, a tailor-shop, a shoemaker's shop, a carpenter's, a smithy; here he wrought his raw materials to the needs of his establishment. And it was when he put on his "plain blue coat, white cassimer waistcoat, black breeches and boots" to visit the fields and the mill, his usual custom in the forenoon, that he was most truly the producer, and most contented.

The estate he divided into five farms, each under an overseer responsible to the manager of the estate, and each equipped with the necessary complement of labor, buildings and stock. Through the manager the reports of progress from the five farms were passed up to the master in the big house every Saturday morning, and with scrupulous precision he transcribed and classified them. Washington never heard of a microbe, nor studied chemistry, yet in these reports and his own conclusions will be found exhaustive experiments in inoculating the soil and rotating crops. He balanced his cultivation so as to produce sufficient food for his people and stock, and the utmost yield of negotiable grains. "Our lands," he wrote, "were originally very good; but use and abuse have made them quite otherwise"—and so he sent abroad for new seeds to try out. Selected quantities of his grains he set aside for experiment upon the diet of his livestock. Although he was a host of lavish hospitality within the house, every move he made as a farmer was a lesson in conservation. His woodcutters got explicit orders to select the timber they cut; his overseers were told not to try to squeeze the land for high crop yield at the expense of upkeep; each new herd of cattle must be better stock than the last; the mill was re-engineered to grind more meal from each bushel of corn; a stone deposit became a quarry; the waters of the Potomac gave up "a sufficiency of fish for my own people" in the first catch, and beyond that a great supply for salting and sale in the winter market; every by-product of the estate was developed and applied. Jefferson sat at Monticello above nature's workshop as at a play; Washington took off his plain blue coat and tinkered with the machinery to increase its efficiency.

In his admirable work on Mount Vernon, Paul Wilstach has hit upon the secret of its master's enthusiasm:

"Mount Vernon was eventually brought to a state of high productiveness, but the scale of life there was such that rarely did the farms show a balance wholly on the right side of the ledger. Washington had to look to his estate for other assets than appeared in the physical valuation of its produce. He found its true and largest asset in the fulfilled ideal of private life; in solving the interesting problems of the planter; in mental health and physical strength; and in the enjoyment of the easy and graceful social life of the colonial country gentleman, of which Mount Vernon became a veritable example."

A vigorous life is easy and natural to a man of Washington's physical power. He was six-feet-three-inches high, rose with the sun, and went to bed at nine unless there were guests. His routine during the sixteen years preceding the Revolution was varied on this day to ride "Valiant" or "Ajax" after the hounds, on that to dine at Belvoir or Gunston Hall, or Belle Aire; now up-river to a dance at Alexandria, now down-river shooting ducks; this week to Annapolis and the races, next to Williamsburg on affairs of the legislature. A never-ending procession of guests arrived and departed, from parsons to British naval officers, and found a uniformly perfect welcome—even extending to the gentleman who "contrary to all expectation" held Washington motionless for three sittings while he painted his first portrait, and charged him slightly more than £57 for effigies of himself, Mrs. Washington, Martha and Jack Custis.

To the refurnished home Mrs. Washington had brought many objects of her own to add to its luxury, which was further enhanced from time to time by orders upon his London agents for furniture and ornaments. On one occasion he wrote for busts of Alexander, Caesar, Charles XII of Sweden and the King of Prussia, fifteen inches high; Prince Eugene and the Duke of Marlborough, somewhat smaller; and "Wild Beasts, not to exceed twelve inches in height nor eighteen in length." He received instead:

> "A Groupe of Aeneas carrying his Father out of Troy, with four statues, viz. his Father Anchises, his wife Creusa and his son Ascanius, neatly finisht and bronzed with copper.. £3.3"
>
> "Two Groupes, with two statues each of Bacchus & Flora, finisht neat & bronzed with copper.. £4.4"

and "Two Lyons after the antique Lyons in Italy," also "finisht neat," with the following apology:

> "There is no busts of Alexander ye Great (none at all of Charles 12th of Sweden), Julius Causar, King of Prussia, Prince Eugene, nor the Duke of Marlborough, of the size desired; and to make models would be very expensive—at least 4 guineas each."

With other orders the agents had better luck, for it was neither difficult nor distasteful to satisfy a Virginia gentleman who merely described the articles ordered (if he described them at all) as either "good" or "neat" or "fashionable." He bought the best, rarely specified price, and paid in the best tobacco—a fair deal all round, and a very agreeably furnished home Mount Vernon became.

There came a day when he was called to command the army in the north. For eight years thereafter Mount Vernon saw him but twice, and then for fleeting visits: once on his way southward from Dobbs Ferry to Williamsburg, during the march on Yorktown; once on his return to the north. Those years had seen his ascent to the height of public veneration. On December 4 of 1783 his officers bade him a frankly tearful good-bye at Fraunce's Tavern in New York, and the chief "walked in silence to Whitehall, followed by a vast procession . . . and entered a barge . . . on his way to lay his commission at the feet of Congress at Annapolis." His progress to Mount Vernon was a succession of popular demonstrations. And when on Christmas Eve he went up the hill and pandemonium broke loose to see the master returned, in his mind were no thoughts of consulates or dictatorships, empire or world-domination, but only profound relief that he had come at last into sweet and voluntary exile from affairs.

He had served without pay through the war, and his first concern now was to put the estate on its feet. He took up the flags of the eastern piazza, reinforced the foundations of the house, "removed two pretty large and full-grown lilacs to the No. Garden gate," combed the neighboring forest for handsome trees to transplant, amplified his orchards, stocked a deer park, and made his daily rounds of the farms. The man who had lately dictated terms to the best soldiers out of Europe got from his gardener a promise to stay sober most of the time on consideration of "four dollars at Christmas, with which he may be drunk four days and four nights; two dollars at Easter to effect the same purpose; two dollars at Whitsuntide to be drunk for two days; a dram in the morning and a drink of grog at dinner at noon."

If there had been visitors before the war, double their number flocked to him now. One night he was routed out of bed to receive a young French sculptor, sent by Jefferson and Franklin in Paris to make his statue for the capitol at Richmond. A Mount Vernon tradition says that a few days later Washington was called out to look at a pair of horses offered for sale. He asked the price, and was told "a thousand dollars." He drew himself up in indignation, for a thousand dollars was an outrageous price for a horse and was likewise a tenth of his whole year's living expense. Houdon, the sculptor, had been dogging Washington's footsteps for days, studying his subject. He caught the general in the fine glow of dignified wrath, cried out, "I 'ave him! I 'ave him!" and set to work at once to make the pose immortal. With a life mask, sketches, and full measurements he returned to Paris, and there, with Gouverneur Morris posing for the standing figure, he made the composite statue which stands at Richmond today.

There came a youngster of twenty, very quiet and abashed at an audience with the great general. This boy's name was Robert Fulton, he who later invented the steamboat. There came Noah Webster, who was to write the great American dictionary; there came Jedediah Morse, who wrote the first American geography. Lafayette, the "French boy," was always welcome, and he spent nineteen days there in the autumn of 1784. Others were not so welcome: "My house may be compared to a well-resorted tavern," wrote Washington. He had to summon young Laurence Washington to Mount Vernon to carry its social burden after candle-light, when he withdrew to his study to answer letters, or to taste the human pleasure of postponing answers "until tomorrow evening," as he confessed to his former secretary of war. But, welcome or uninvited, they all came, for the country was to have a new government, and Washington was not only to help build it, but to run it. With the same modest misgivings of his own capacity for the post that he had frankly confessed in 1775, he went out again in 1789 to serve his country, and put aside again the labor that was nearest to his heart.

For eight years more his sight of Mount Vernon was limited to visits borrowed from public affairs, but he never lost his grip on its minute arrangements, directing, advising, correcting in his letters to his managers. In one downright homesick moment he said flatly that he would rather be at home with a friend or two than to be attended at the seat of government by the officers of state and the representatives of every power in Europe. John Adams, after his inauguration in 1797, wrote a letter to his wife, who had not been there to enjoy the greatest moment of his life. "It was made more affecting to me," he said, "by the presence of the General, whose countenance was as serene and unclouded as the day. He seemed to enjoy a triumph over me. Methought I heard him say, 'Ay, I am fairly out and you fairly in! See which of us will be the happiest!'" Everything on that bright March day in Philadelphia sang "Home!"

Presently he was there, admiring the new setting of the fine furniture and silver and glassware and china brought down from the Presidential Mansion in the Capital, some of which is in the house today. Sixty-five years old, with the western world at his feet, and he saw only the broad reaches of the Potomac down below the ha-ha walls. Sixty-six, and to see a young lad named Charles Carroll from Maryland courting his favorite grand-daughter made a man feel young himself. Sixty-seven, forty years married, the favorite grand-daughter to be married (though not to Charles Carroll), and life seemed perennial. One December morning he caught cold riding the farms, and two days later was dead.

Nothing short of the domestic enthusiasm of George Washington could have kept Mount Vernon in order. For sixty years it yielded gradually to the advance of time. Then, through the truly heroic zeal of Miss Ann Pamela Cunningham of Laurens, S. C., and the eloquence of Edward Everett, and the fine spirit of Miss Cunningham's Mount Vernon Ladies' Association of the Union, the estate was purchased, and with searching fidelity to the wishes of its master, restored to the state in which he would have had it. Too fulsome praise can hardly be expressed—certainly not here—for the good sense, discrimination and good organization which combine to maintain the estate. It is as if a hand had touched it lightly on a spring morning in the brightest year of its occupancy, and had held it, fixed forever in the pose, like the castle of the sleeping princess. No prince will come to rouse the place. But better than that, after sixty years of care and a century and a half of life, it re-creates each year to thousands of pilgrims the crises and victories that wrote our creed as a nation. And fortunately no landholder on this great farm of ours will leave Mount Vernon without a deep sense of relief that it is first and last a perfect monument to a country gentleman.

THE QUINCY HOMESTEAD

THE QUINCY HOUSE

which sheltered, among other delicate ornaments, three successive Dorothy Quincys. There are ever so many things in the house today to call up a Quincy tradition, for if you scratch almost any chapter of New England history you will find a Quincy tradition underneath. Take away its Hoars, Lowells, Holmeses, Adamses, Wendells, Hancocks, Sewalls—to mention only a few of the Quincy connections—and what, indeed, becomes of New England?

The Quincy Homestead

IT is perhaps impolite to compare a Massachusetts family tree to a banyan instead of the conventional elm, but no prowler among her old houses can come away without a feeling that almost everything in New England is related to almost everything else. Chicago glances over Boston's shoulder and finds her reading the Monday *Transcript's* genealogy page; Chicago howls with laughter and turns to *Vanity Fair* to see what is going on in New York. Boston is momentarily interrupted, doesn't know quite what Chicago is laughing at, returns a well-bred smile of complete detachment, and plunges back into the genealogy page.

This business of keeping track of marriages and deaths, cousinships and children-by-the-second-wife is serious, though bred of no spirit of arrogance, no desire to find a coat of arms for the door of the new town-car. There is brisk mental exercise in chasing an obscure ancestor to his lair and finding that he was what you thought he was when you started out, and not his own grand-nephew-twice-removed. Further, reasons Boston, unless you know to whom a person is related, how can you know to whom that person is related? By this sound process of logic a personal news item in a Boston newspaper worth six agate lines of white paper is so interestingly overgrown with eighteen or twenty lines of genealogical wistaria that the outsider has some trouble peering through the vines to the item itself. He will never understand the irrelevant matter until he understands that it is not irrelevant, that the ever-present landmarks of tradition are bristling with precedents, and that the respect for those precedents is so congenital that they guide the footsteps of New Englanders more than even New Englanders suspect.*

If the foreigner from beyond the Hudson or the Delaware or the Mississippi will do himself the favor of visiting the Quincy house, he will sense the point, and be paid in full measure by the contemplation of a house with a varied and engaging story.

It began life as a Puritan farmstead, by a brookside in the town of Braintree. Sixteen years after the first settlement at Plymouth, and therefore nearly three centuries ago, William Coddington built three rooms on a kitchen. Bigoted public opinion soon broke up the trio of liberals who used to sit and talk free worship before the great fireplace in that kitchen—Coddington fled, Sir Harry Vane went other ways, and Anne Hutchinson was banished from the colony. Edmund Quincy, the new owner, came out from Boston, with a retinue of six servants. Such a staff was a rare luxury in those ascetic days. It is partially explained by the fact that in an age of large families Edmund Quincy's was no exception, and four children wanted a lot of looking after. He enlarged the house to accommodate his growing tribe, and about 1685 gave up the Coddington structure to his slaves, while he built a new house a few rods away. (It was this Edmund's sister who married the master of the Mint, John Hull; he named Point Judith after her, and their daughter Hannah was the maiden who was given in marriage with a dowry of her weight in pine-tree shillings—one hundred and twenty-five pounds avoirdupois and five hundred sterling.)

* I am told by Mr. George Stephenson, of the *Transcript*, that the bulk of special subscription to the genealogical issues comes from the Middle West. Again brutal statistics blunder in to shatter a pleasant theory. I repeat this to a Boston beldame; she says, "Why of course—those subscribers are from families who migrated west to make money, and *now*, of course—" and leaves me to fill out the sentence. My theory stands, and defies the lightnings.

THE QUINCY HOMESTEAD

Another Edmund, the third of the American line and the second in possession of the estate on Quincy Brook, fell heir to it when his father died in 1698. Through his grandmother Edmund was already related to the line which was presently to bring forth John Adams. His thirteen brothers and sisters and numerous cousins connected him by marriage with nearly all the families of the settlement, and out of one of those ceremonies is left to us a glimpse of tragedy: Judge Sewall records in his diary that just after "Cousin Daniel" was being married to Mrs. Shepard, when the guests were singing in the hall, one of them dropped dead. Her body was carried to the room which was to have been the bride's, "the Bridegroom and Bride . . . going away like Persons put to flight in Battel" to spend their honeymoon at a neighbor's house.

Edmund the Third was a man not only of fortune but of discrimination, which he showed by marrying Dorothy Flynt—the first "Dorothy Q." In 1706 he invited the whole countryside to the estate by the brook, and around and above the old Coddington house the whole corps of neighbors, abetted by hard cider, raised the huge timbers of a new mansion, the one which stands there today restored to its full dignity. It was a suitable dwelling for a man of eminence in the colony, a man big enough to quarrel with Benning Wentworth over the boundary of New Hampshire. On the rear of the new home he built an extension containing a bedroom and a study, where "Tutor" Flynt, Mrs. Quincy's brother, could find rest from his duties in Harvard College, and there Tutor Flynt spent most of a crusty, tobacco-perfumed bachelor life as a sort of paying guest, driving down to Braintree from Cambridge in a calèche for week-ends and the longer holidays. (Tutor Flynt, by the way, is the earliest recorded user of the "If-you-are-going-to-Heaven-I-don't-want-to-go-there" joke, though genuine research would doubtless reveal that Shem made the same remark to Japheth one afternoon when the Ark lay becalmed.)

The light of the household was Dorothy Q, and the source of her radiance was her family of growing children. Three of them claim our attention: Edmund (the Fourth), who inherited the Homestead; Josiah (the first of a series of notable Josiahs); and a second Dorothy, whom her grandson, Oliver Wendell Holmes, described in this way:

> "O Damsel Dorothy! Dorothy Q!
> Strange is the gift that I owe to you;
> Such a gift as never a king
> Save to daughter or son might bring,—
> All my tenure of heart and hand,
> All my title to house and land;
> Mother and sister and child and wife
> And joy and sorrow and death and life!
>
> "What if a hundred years ago
> Those close-shut lips had answered No,
> When forth the tremulous question came
> That cost the maiden her Norman name
> Should I be I, or would it be
> One-tenth another to nine-tenths me?"

Dorothy Q the Second was a dear child, carrying at fifteen the cares of the household, and apparently pointed down the path of a winsome spinsterhood. But within a few weeks, in the summer of 1737, [her grandmother, her mother, and then her father died, and she married Edward Jackson and went to live in Boston, where her husband was a ship-owner in partnership with her brother Josiah.

One of their vessels, the *Bethell*, with thirty-seven men and fourteen guns, fell in with the *Jesus Maria and Joseph*, a Spaniard with 110 men and twenty-six guns. The *Bethell's* skipper gambled on the gathering twilight, set up six wooden dummy guns, hung sailors' caps and hats in the rigging to suggest a numerous crew, and then demanded the Spaniard's surrender. Down came her ensign! The Spanish crew was set ashore at Fayal, and the *Bethell* brought back to Josiah and Dorothy one-hundred-and-sixty-one chests of silver, and two of Spanish gold.

With the prize money safely banked, Josiah was able to retire from business at the age of forty. He moved to Braintree, taking up his residence in the Hancock parsonage, across the way from the Homestead. Brother Edmund, the lantern-jawed parson, who had been living in Boston and spending his summers in Braintree, moved to the Homestead in his turn, lost most of his share of the prize money in artless speculation, and turned to farming.

Life in the two families presented diversion aplenty—most of the eligible young men of Boston and Braintree were courting Edmund's five daughters. A sober young man named John Adams was running perilously close to the charms of Hannah, Josiah's daughter. He was a marked man when her cousins, Esther and Susan, suddenly "broke in upon Hannah and me and interrupted a conversation that would have terminated in a courtship that would have terminated in a marriage which might have depressed me to absolute poverty and obscurity to the end of my life." He veered, took a deep breath, went away from there, and two years later was married to Abigail Smith, who alone of American women was the wife and the mother of an American president. Important guests occasionally penetrated the swarm of suitors—such men as Admiral Warren and Sir William Pepperrell, the heroes of Louisburg; or Benjamin Franklin, who sent Squire Quincy cuttings of Rhenish grapevines and a new stove which he had invented; or Sir Harry Frankland, who gave the Squire a fine pear-sapling—the same Sir Harry who married Agnes Surriage, whom he had first seen barefoot, scrubbing floors in a tavern in Marblehead.

And the youngest of all was Dorothy Q the Third, with four big brothers and three boy cousins to pay her court, and four elder sisters to study. Through all the bitter period that followed the Boston Massacre, when her cousin Josiah Junior and John Adams were defending the British captain, and her cousin Samuel was appearing for the Crown, Dorothy Q was on the fringe of the excitement, coquetting with all of the earnest youths who were polishing their arms, but engaging in entangling alliance with none. Not until she was twenty-seven did she make her choice, and then it was John Hancock, the chief figure of pre-revolutionary days in Boston, a vigorous patriot who defied the Crown and became a member of the Committee of Safety. Most of the winter of 1774–75 she spent with his aunt in the Hancock mansion, where came Revere, and Warren, and Samuel and John Adams. By March of '75 she was back in Quincy, gathering her trousseau, and superintending the application of a new French wall-paper to the walls of the north parlor, where a company of conventional blue Venuses and Cupids, garlanded with delicate flowers, was to preside over the wedding ceremony. The untroubled Homestead presented a strong contrast to the one she had left in Boston: a loyalist rabble stormed the Hancock house, tore down the fence, broke the windows and wrecked the coach-house, and the prospective bridegroom, threatened with arrest, was obliged to escape with little dignity and all possible speed.

He turned up at Concord for the meeting of the Provincial Congress on April 15, and after its adjournment he was joined by Dorothy, Madame Hancock and Samuel Adams at the Rev. Jonas Clark's house in Lexington. Quietly, in the evening of the eighteenth, British troops assembled in Boston for a march to destroy the stores at Concord. As quietly, Paul Revere rowed across the mouth of the river to Charlestown, slipped by the guard, and rode hell-bent into the sleeping country. He pulled up at the Clark parsonage and called for Adams and Hancock. "Don't make so much noise," said a minute-man on guard. "*Noise!*" shouted Revere, "You'll have noise enough before long—the regulars are coming!"—and he delivered Joseph Warren's warning to Adams and Hancock to get out of the neighborhood at once. Against their will they fled to Woburn, while Dorothy slept no more that night. At dawn she saw Pitcairn and his scarlet column tramp to the Lexington common and set fire to the Revolution. Then she joined her lover in Woburn, and when he tried to forbid her to go back to Boston, the strain of a sleepless night and the horrors of the day broke the bridle on her tongue and she tossed her head and retorted: "Recollect, Mr. Hancock, I am not under your control yet. I shall go to my father tomorrow!"

Having spoken her mind, she exercised a woman's privilege in changing it—and did almost as he had asked: set out at once for a safe refuge at Fairfield in Connecticut.

She was still somewhat piqued. She found at Fairfield, in the person of her host's nephew, an eager listener to her narrative of the skirmish at Lexington—a Princeton graduate who was studying law. He probably gained her confidence at once by asking her just what she thought he ought to do, and by offering to join the colors for her sake. Aaron Burr was very accomplished at that sort of thing, and considered it good exercise, for he was carrying on two other affairs and an anonymous sentimental correspondence at the same time. To Hancock's affectionate letter from Philadelphia Dorothy made no reply. For the peace offering of silk stockings he sent her she said not even "thank-you." Then either Madame Hancock or Dorothy's own conscience stepped in and settled the quarrel. Burr left for Cambridge to enlist, and Hancock came to Fairfield and married the lady.

They took up their home in Boston on the heels of the British evacuation, and until Hancock went back to Braintree to die in 1793 her life was a brilliant panorama of illustrious society. When Washington came to Boston in 1789, Hancock, who was governor of the Commonwealth, invited him to be a guest in the fine house on Beacon Street opposite the Common. Washington declined and the governor offered him an invitation to dinner. On the assumption that within his own state a governor's position was sovereign to that of the President, he did not call upon Washington before dinner. The hour came, but no President, and Hancock sent a messenger to apologize to Washington for not having paid his respects, and to plead that sudden illness prevented. Washington guessed that the illness was sour-grape poisoning and ate his dinner at home. Later in the evening the lieutenant-governor and two councilmen appeared to repeat Hancock's apology. "I informed them," Washington writes in his diary, "that I should not see the governor except at my own lodgings." The next day Hancock bent his stiff neck to the president, apologized, and the two became friends again.

The Squire had long since sold his rights in the old Homestead, though the family continued to occupy it until his death in 1788. It passed successively through the families of Black, Greenleaf, and Woodward, and then into the hands of the town of Quincy, which was now formally detached from Braintree. For thirty years it was held by the town as part of a trust fund Ebenezer Woodward left to found a girl's academy to match the boy's school started by John Adams.

THE QUINCY HOMESTEAD

Even before the Squire's family had dispersed from the house, its earlier liveliness was somewhat dimmed by the crescent line of able Quincys in another Quincy house built by the first Josiah, and now known as the "later Quincy Mansion." From its windows he recorded the sailing of the British from Boston in 1775; from those windows his children saw the *Constitution* sail in victorious over the *Guerriere*. There lived Josiah the Second, agent of the provincials at London, who died off Marblehead as the firing at Lexington began, while his wife and the third Josiah were fleeing from a threatened naval attack on Braintree. Josiah the Third grew up to be mayor of Boston and president of Harvard, and if no other distinction remained to him except this passage from his speech in Congress on the embargo in 1808, it would be a proud enough monument for any American:

> "But I shall be told, 'This may lead to war.' I ask, 'Are we now at peace?' Certainly not, unless retiring from insult be peace—unless shrinking under the lash be peace. The surest way to prevent war is not to fear it. The idea that nothing on earth is so dreadful as war is inculcated too studiously among us. Disgrace is worse. Abandonment of essential rights is worse."

Is it any wonder that Daniel Webster, Lafayette, and the Adamses, father and son, came often to the home of Josiah, or that, given his heredity and achievement, he had such sons as Josiah the Fourth, another mayor of Boston and an able economist, and Edmund, the stanch abolitionist?

The older house by the brook was leading a humble and retired old age when the Colonial Dames took over its custody. Their restoration not only has made the utmost of the material they found, but has brought to the house a collection of articles which are uniformly good and are in some instances rare and beautiful. The long hall has tall spotless wainscoting and hunting paper, a carven balustrade and newel post; in a low-studded dining-room a set of 1770 Dutch chairs surrounds an Empire table, in a corner stands a buffet whose builder died a century and a half ago; at the fireplace are Delft tiles nearly as aged as the fireplace itself, and there is an odd Chinese paper on the walls. In the parlor is the Venus-and-Cupid paper hung for Dorothy Q's wedding, in the window frames is glass made by a Quincy in the first glassworks in America. You may read in one of those panes the initials "J H" as you may find the writer's full name on the Declaration of Independence, and in the pane below, in the same hand, "You I love, and you alone." You will be interested in Tutor Flynt's bed, built in a recess of the brookside bedroom. You may be mildly thrilled by the Indian-proof shutters, mystified by the secret staircase which follows the course of the chimney, and delighted with the kitchen William Coddington built, with its eight-inch beams, Dutch oven, churn, spinning-wheel, and a musket over the mantel for inviting Indians to dinner.

There are ever so many things in the house today to call up a Quincy tradition, for if you scratch almost any chapter of New England history you will find a Quincy tradition underneath. Take away its Hoars, Lowells, Holmeses, Adamses, Wendells, Hancocks, Sewalls—to mention only a few of the Quincy connections—and you have left hardly enough to make a Monday *Transcript*.

And yet their generic importance was the least of their concerns. "Could I ever suppose," wrote John Adams, "that family pride were in any way excusable, I should think a descent from a line of vigorous independent New England farmers for a hundred years was a better foundation for it than a descent through royal or noble scoundrels ever since the flood."

The Timothy Dexter Mansion

THE TIMOTHY DEXTER MANSION

Over in a corner of the garden stood an Indian chieftain, next to him William Pitt, and beyond the two the martial figure of General Morgan. The Goddess of Fame, Louis XVI, John Jay, the King of Russia, Solomon, Venus, the Governor of New Hampshire—these were a few of the forty "immortals," in his garden of celebrities. In a prominent position stood a portrait in pine of Lord Dexter himself, labeled "I am the greatest man in the EAST."

THE TIMOTHY DEXTER MANSION

> Lord Dexter is a man of fame;
> Most celebrated is his name;
> More precious far than gold that's pure,
> Lord Dexter shine for evermore.
> —*Jonathan Plummer.*

YES, Jonathan Plummer wrote that jingle. It is from the only survivor of a gross of eulogies he wrote of Lord Dexter. And quite proper that he should. He was Lord Dexter's poet laureate, hired, clothed and fed to produce eulogies on demand. His poetry was awful, and the tragedy is that he knew it. Said he didn't like to read too much good verse because it made his own look sorry. But when a man has given up peddling fish and racy European pamphlets in order to study for the ministry, and neither the ministry nor the melodrama pays, he can't be blamed, especially if he has the appetite of an ox and the soul of a poet, for going to work for anyone as poet laureate. Lord Dexter outfitted him in a long black cloak with gold stars on the lapels, and fringe, and a black under dress, a huge cocked hat, and a gold-headed cane. There was a great row about the fringe: Jonathan refused to wear it, Lord Dexter pooh-poohed. *Pooh-poohed a poet laureate!* Still, Maecenas was Maecenas: Jonathan wore the fringe.

Timothy Dexter was a leather-dresser, born in Malden in 1743. Treating leather to simulate "morocco" was a new art, which he mastered, and which, on account of the demand for "morocco" for women's shoes, built him a nice fortune. He married a thrifty widow, who had a little huckster business of her own. They emerged from the period of the Revolution with a son and daughter, and a few thousand dollars. Continental money had dropped to two-and-sixpence on the pound, and the securities of Massachusetts issued to support the money had tumbled to the same depths. John Hancock and Thomas Russel, Bostonians of large fortunes, bought in many of these securities to oblige their friends and to hearten the public's morale, which was as low as its money. Timothy Dexter heard of it, and risked every loose dollar he had in the same investment. Then Hamilton's funding system went into operation and made him a wealthy man, who need never dress another hide as long as he lived.

He had gambled that the United States Constitution was a fixture, and he had won. He played more money on the same color, and won again and again. Charlestown, still convalescing from a severe fire, was not to the liking of this new-laid magnate. He moved to Newburyport, after Salem and Boston the busiest port in the Commonwealth. He bought two fine estates, occupied one for a short time, and then moved to the other. As the property of a prominent merchant it had been one of the fine houses of a community of steady, prosperous people, whose philosophy was drawn from the Old Testament, education from the Three R's, and deportment from a rigid Puritan ancestry. Into its complacent calm Timothy Dexter came bellowing like a bull in a china shop, and proceeded to build the china shop about him.

You may have wondered about the source of the iron-dog-and-Diana tendency on the lawns of our captains of industry. It dates from Lord Dexter, and in justice to him it should be said that he set a mark that neither posterity nor Adolphus Busch nor Carl Hagenbeck nor Ex-Senator Clark could begin to approach. They may have paid more for their cupolas and summer-houses and plaster-of-Paris bubchen, but Timothy Dexter, the self-made lord, leather-dresser, landscape gardener and architect, finished the race with a permanent world's record before they were born. He took a square colonial house of straight and dignified proportions, polished it with bright paint, and set gilt balls and railings and minarets upon its roof, till from the sea it looked like a Christmas tree gone mad. There was a magnificent garden between the house and the highway, full of flowers and fruit that were the envy of a community of husbandmen, but mere nature was not allowed to go on unassisted.

"Hear me, good Lord," he wrote. "I am agoing to let your children know now, good Lord, what has been in the world a great ways back—not old Plymouth, but stop to Adam and Eve."

Accordingly there rose in the garden clusters of single columns, and groups of wooden arches, about fifteen feet high, and presently the astonished natives of Newburyport saw them capped with wooden effigies. Before the main doorway was a Roman arch, and upon it, reading from left to right, John Adams, George Washington, Thomas Jefferson—all life size, with John Adams uncovered because Dexter would not permit anyone to stand at Washington's right with his hat on. Jefferson he thought was a trifle obscure, so he engaged an artist to paint "Declaration of Independence" upon the scroll in its author's wooden hand. The artist had lashed himself to the column, had spaced the lettering, and had painted the letters "DEC-," when Lord Timothy, squinting up from below, remarked:

"That's not the way to spell 'Constitution'!"

"You don't want the Constitution," called the artist. "You want 'Declaration of Independence'!"

"I want 'Constitution'!" roared Dexter. "and 'Constitution' I will have!"

His recollection of the Declaration of Independence was foggy, but he knew that he had made most of his money by the adhesive properties of the Constitution, and he was not going back on his talisman now. The artist refused to make the statue ridiculous, and Dexter charged into the house, charged out with a loaded pistol, and as the artist left across-country, fired, missed the artist—but hit the house.

Over in a corner of the garden stood an Indian chieftain, next to him William Pitt, and beyond the two the martial figure of General Morgan. Morgan was not quite satisfactory, so a few coats of paint made him over into Bonaparte. The Goddess of Fame, Louis XVI, John Jay, the King of Russia, Solomon, Venus, the Governor of New Hampshire—these were a few of the forty "immortals" in his garden of celebrities. In a prominent position stood a portrait in pine of Lord Dexter himself, labeled "I am the greatest man in the EAST." Four lions, two *couchant*, two *passant*, stood guard beside him to prove it. This caption originally included the North, South and West, and what sudden access of modesty caused him to censor it is a buried secret. When the hurricane of 1815 toppled most of the figures from their pinnacles, they were sold at auction. Pitt brought one dollar, Fame five, the Traveling Preacher fifty cents, the Indian chief was set up in a cornfield to scare crows, and Lord Timothy, the greatest man in the East, found no bidders. That is fame.

His gallery was the product of expert wood-carvers in Newburyport and Salem, men who were turning out creditable work for the figureheads of the vast merchant fleet that made Salem a port known round the world. It cost him not a cent less than $15,000, twice the price he paid for the estate. Upon the interior of the house he lavished the same attention, and imported from France the last word in flamboyant furniture, voluptuous draperies, and generally meretricious *objets d'art*. His agents had more taste than he, to be sure, but if a worthy piece found its way into the house, it was sure to be stained and damaged in the next carouse. In his business dealings with Hancock and Russel he had caught glimpses of their libraries, and it occurred to him that the greatest man in the East should own fine books, so he bought them by the linear yard in costly bindings. He rarely read them, and guests relieved him of the finer engravings with which they were illustrated. In the same way he filled the house with paintings, which were so bad that not even his guests cared to steal them. The dearest of all his hobbies was a collection of clocks and watches. Once a week they were set running and regulated; each day he visited them all, and gave a word of encouragement or censure to each, from the great Dutch fellow who prophesied approaching rain, to the daintiest enameled chronometer in the hilt of a French fan. The fruits and blossoms of his garden were as keen a source of satisfaction to him as they were to the maidens and urchins of the town. After a few experimental visits had revealed the clumsy vulgarity of his attentions to all women, nice girls never went to see Dexter's museum. To the small boy, however, he was the personification of all that was grand and fantastic; furthermore, they could scent his berries and plums and melons for a radius of five miles, no matter which way the wind blew.

It is quite right to assume that even a successful speculation in government paper could hardly finance the upkeep of such an outrageously extravagant menâge. Where did the money come from?

Everyone in New England, as his notoriety spread, asked the same question. The most picturesque reply is from his own pen—a chapter from a tract called "Pickle for the Knowing Ones," which he wrote and published, and which, with a few italicized explanatory notes, follows:

HOW DID TIMOTHY DEXTER GET HIS MONEY ye (*he*) says: bying whale bone for staing (*staying*) for ships . in grosing (*gross*) three hundred & 40 tons—bort all in boston, salum and all in Noue york, under Cover . oppenly told them for my ships; they all laffed. so I had at my oan pris. I had four Counning men for Rounners; thay found the horne, as I told them to act the fool . I was full of Cash . I had nine tun of silver on hand at that time— all that time the Creaters (*creatures*) more or less laffing. it spread very fast . here is the Rub—in fifty days thay smelt a Rat—found where it was gone to Nouebry Port—spekkelaters swarming like hell houns—to be short with it I made seventey five per sent—one tun and a halfe of silver on hand and over—

one more spect—Drole a Nuf—I Dreamed of warming pans three nites; that they would doue in the west inges (*Indies*) . (*He did not dream this, but was put up to it by the chaffing of a group of mischievous ship-clerks about the Port. Warming pans were about as necessary in the West Indies as coals in Newcastle.*) I got no more than fortey two thousand—put them in nine vessels for difrent ports. that tuck good hold. (*It did: to the astonishment of New England, the warming pans were found to be excellent utensils in which to roast coffee, and the lids equally useful in skimming hot sugar syrup.*) I cleared sevinty nine per sent . the pans thay made use of them for Coucking—blessed good in Deade (*indeed*) missey (*monsieur*) got nise handel—very good masser ("*Massa*") for Coukey (*cooking; he*

THE TIMOTHY DEXTER MANSION

here reproduces the dialect of the French and British West Indian negroes.) Now burn my fase the best thing I Ever see in borne days I found I was very luckky in spekkelation.

I Dreamed that the good book was Run Down in this Countrey nine years gone, so low as halfe prise and Dull at that—the bibel I means . I had the Ready Cash . by holl sale I bort twelve per sent under halfe pris: thay cost fortey one sents Each bibbel—twentey one thousand—I put them into twenty one vessels for the west inges and sent a text that all of them must have one bibel in every family, or if not thay would goue to hell—and if thay had Dun wiked, flie to the bibel and on thare Neas and kiss the bibel three times and look up to heaven annest (*and ask*) for forgivnes, my Captteins all had Compleat orders—here Coms the good luck: I made one hundred per sent & littel over. then I found I had made money anuf. I hant (*haven't*) speckalated sence old time. by government secourities I made forty seven thousands Dolors—that is the old afare. Now I toald the all, the sekrett. Now be still, let me A lone; Dont wonder Noe more houe I got my money, boaz (*boys*).

If there were space it could be devoted to his successful corner of the opium market, to his land speculations, and to other sounder investments, such as the Essex Merrimack bridge, which kept his coffers full. But there is not, if we are to have a glimpse of the motley crew who fawned about him and lived at his expense. Plummer, the poet laureate and jingle-monger we have seen, Plummer, who told Dexter that the Druids crowned their laureates with mistletoe, and whom Dexter duly crowned, amidst great ceremony, with parsley, there being no mistletoe in the garden. Then there was a Newburyport schoolmaster who fell out of the graces of the town because he took his pupils to walk in the fields and taught them the names of the birds and flowers, used charts and globes in geography lessons, performed simple chemical experiments which the parents soundly suspected were tricks, and believed in the lecture system more than in the birch rod. With a smattering of astronomy and a fertile imagination this man attached himself to Dexter in the capacity of astrologer and chief confidant. He was probably in league with Madam Hooper and Moll Pitcher, two seeresses of rich local reputation, for Dexter often called upon them to solve his future. There was Burley, called Dwarf Billy, a giant wrestler who stood six-feet-and-seven-inches in his socks when he wore them; Dexter hired him as a sort of watchman, porter and body-guard, to do his fighting for him. It was Dwarf Billy whom Dexter called upon to put a tipsy sea-captain off the place, after he had wagered that no two men Dexter had could put him out. Looking up to Burley's summit, the sailor put his guinea in his lordship's hands, saying: "By Jupiter, if this is your dwarf, how big are your giants?"

Hogarth never drew a stranger company. It was downright Elizabethan in its romantic depravity. Barred from the company of intelligent, modest people by the pride which would not permit him to play the hypocrite, Dexter brought his society to him, and cared very little about its ancestry, so long as it gave him adulation and echoed his tipsy amiability. The house was infested with shady adventurers and blowzy females from the ports, come to gather a little money and pass on; no fine day went by but travelers came to see this remarkable man at close hand, to flatter him, to hear him tell the story of conferring upon himself the title of "Lord"; to carry some souvenir of his tireless eccentricity back to the folks at home, and you may believe that it lost nothing in the telling. The riff-raff of the town attended a funeral which he advertised in his honor, and

THE TIMOTHY DEXTER MANSION

which he watched from behind the curtains of an upper window while a heavy mahogany coffin he had bought was borne to the summer house where he expected some day to rest. He was annoyed that his epileptic son, being drunk enough to weep lavishly, was the only one who mourned, and that Plummer did not put enough genuine fire into the funeral oration.

Once in a while a visitor crossed him, and he rushed to the house for a pistol; one such adventure cost him a term in the Ipswich gaol, though his aim was so poor that he never hit anyone. For a time he held public office, that of "informer of deer," which carried the duty of arousing the town when deer were seen in the vicinity. Even the beasts of the wilderness laughed at him—no deer ever ventured near during his term. With books to read but no mind to read them with, his wife long since fled from his home, his son half-mad and his daughter wholly so, Dexter, feigning a feverish interest in affairs of which he knew absolutely nothing, became an object of contemptuous amusement even to the gypsies of Dogtown who passed his house to peddle berries. Today the rankness and the nearness of him has passed, and it is hard to find for Timothy Dexter any emotion beyond that of profound pity.

He died in 1806 and was buried in a simple grave in a public cemetery. A sensible, methodical will disposed of his property, and the house passed into other hands, which cleared out his forest of statuary, tore down the gilt balls, and took the masquerade costume off the building whose dignity he had so unceremoniously insulted. In the process Timothy Dexter, "Lord" by his own acclamation, has been sunk without trace. The house today is quite the most imposing in a town unusually blessed with Colonial homes, but it is not Dexter's. Dexter is wholly dead.

FAMOUS COLONIAL HOUSES

His greatest work, the "Pickle for the Knowing Ones," must never die. Superlatives can damn it here forever, and any attempt to dissect its philosophy must await the collaboration of a specialist in the psychology of insanity, a student of Chaucerian spelling, and an apostle of tolerance. When those three meet, we shall understand the man. Meanwhile, the "Pickle" is worth reading.

To his second edition he added this postscript:

fouder (*further*) mister Printer the Nowing ones complane of my book the fust edition had no stops I put in A Nuf here and thay may pepper and salt it as thay plese

,,

,,

::

..............................::............

..........................!!!!!!!!!!!!!!!!!!!!!!!!!!!..

..................................!!!!!!!!!!!!!!...

....!!!!!!...

....!...

,,

.............................?????????????????????????..

The Kendall House

THE KENDALL HOUSE

Here Washington and Rochambeau planned the Yorktown campaign. From the upper windows you may look over the roofs of the town where André and Arnold plotted to betray the United States. Across the Hudson you may see the faint outlines of the village of Tappan, where André was held prisoner, and where Washington shared his breakfast with the convicted spy. At the foot of the hill below you is the landing where British dignitaries came to plead for André's life.

THE KENDALL HOUSE

A WHITE house with solid vertigris blinds stands comfortably beside the Post road. There is a little old cannon on the lawn, a sad bell-mouthed field piece with its jaw jutted fiercely out to bark at any British man-o'-war that presumes to come back up the Hudson. A green ridge rises behind the house, setting it off like Wedgwood ware, and a gentle brook idles down the slope toward the river.

Set in a jog of the stone wall at the highway is a memorial tablet which has evidently gone unnoticed by the gentlemen who write histories for primary schools—who are supposed to watch the fires on our national shrines, and to toss a bright epithet, an apt name, or a bit of patriotic tinder on the coals. In missing this Dobbs Ferry house they are clearly guilty of neglect of duty. It has a story that goes clear down to the stuff every American believes he is made of. If we borrow a stock phrase from the supply of the school historian and call this house the "Birthplace of Victory" we shall not be far from the fact, nor serving ill a spot which recalls with rich significance the travail in which our nation was born.

In 1780 there were three invading British armies rooted on the Atlantic coast: Clinton had driven Washington off Manhattan island in 1776 and had already held the city for four years; Cornwallis made Yorktown a base for expeditions into Virginia and the Carolinas, and Tarleton held Charleston. For four years the enemy had hoped to effect a junction between his forces in Canada and those in New York, and the Hudson was to be his highway. For four years Washington had hovered like an eagle over the river, wheeling now into Westchester, now swooping upon Jersey. Inadequately equipped, he dared not take the offensive. He had to be content to wait for the time when Clinton might relax his vigilance upon the city, then to strike, brilliantly and savagely, but the sum of these maneuvers was only to harass the enemy, not to unseat him. Twice since Washington's time has his fortitude been matched in our history: once by Lincoln, and once by Lee. Once, in our own lifetime, it has been equalled by the French nation. It was from France, in 1780, that our relief ultimately came.

After four years of war, with British patrols making frequent raids through Yonkers and over the upper acres of the Philipse estate, with British warships plying up and down the Hudson at will past the silenced batteries of Forts Washington and Lee, with the Cowboys and Skinners of both armies making life wretched throughout the neutral ground in which Dobbs Ferry lay, the village was in ill temper. It lies opposite the northern end of the Palisades, and while the British held New York it was the most southerly ferry safe for American despatch riders from Westchester County to Jersey and the south—a vital link in the chain of communication between the scattered states. So Dobbs Ferry saw plenty of skirmishing. Earthworks were thrown up in the village; the remains of an ancient redoubt may be discovered today after patient search near Broadway and Livingston Avenue, and the Livingston mansion, the most pretentious house in town, asked neither exemption nor privilege and surrounded itself with trenches. No one knew when the enemy might advance in force up the Albany Post Road, and in Dobbs Ferry's 1780-temper, no one proposed to let him march without a fight.

Word had gone through the states that Lafayette, the gay

French lad who came over to fight with Washington, had gone home. "He's young," men said. "It was only a lark for him. He's had enough. 'Leave of absence' was it! 'French leave,' more likely." Lafayette was young, but he had not had enough. How a youth of twenty-two petitioned the court of France for an army, a fleet and a generous loan for the states we need not inquire. He got everything he asked and came back to tell General Washington so and to confer upon him Louis Sixteenth's commission as lieutenant-general of the Armies of France and admiral of His Majesty's Navy.

In 1918 the United States transport Leviathan, seven days out of New York, made the harbor of Brest and set ten thousand fighting men ashore. In the harbor of Newport, Rhode Island, on July 11, 1780 eleven French warships and thirty-two transports, three months out of Brest, set six thousand fighting men of France upon American soil. Ponder on those figures: six thousand men are the complement of two modern regiments, the half of a bitter day's casualty list; six thousand men were the Army of France, the Army of Deliverance. After they had thawed a cool reception, they were welcomed as such, and while the Comte de Rochambeau, at their head, was fêted by the dignitaries of Newport, his disciplined troops pitched their tents in the Rhode Island orchards, and as their commander proudly reported to their King, never even robbed the fruit-trees!

Cumulative bad luck camped down simultaneously on the American cause. Scurvy among the French troops prevented their moving to attack New York. Clinton made a demonstration against them at Newport until Washington frightened him back indoors. Rochambeau found difficulty in conveying his ideas of strategy to American headquarters in Jersey, and it took all of Lafayette's tact to keep the forces in contented alliance. At last, when the summer was nearly gone, Washington arranged a council of war at Hartford.

The operations of the allied armies planned at that conference hinged upon the co-operation of a second French land force and the French fleet. The land force was even then bottled up in Brest by British warships, the French admiral was in the West Indies and showed no signs of coming north. To make matters worse, there was brewing over on the Hudson a plot which Washington later called "one of the severest strokes that could have been meditated against us." It was so well known among the British that it now seems incredible that no hint of warning had filtered through the Neutral Ground to American headquarters. London gossip predicted openly throughout the summer a *coup* which would shortly bring this upstart rebellion to its knees.

One morning in late September four farmer boys from Westchester undertook to watch the Albany post-road north of Tarrytown, and to see that no Tory patrols drove stolen cattle southward. They halted a well-dressed civilian and searched him. In his stockings they found a plan of the fortifications at West Point, an inventory of ammunition, full directions for attacking *and taking* the forts, and a résumé of General Washington's most recent statement of the condition and prospects of the American cause. It was suspicious enough to find these papers on an unknown civilian, but when he proved to be Major John André, adjutant-general of the British Army, and when inspection showed that the last two documents were in the handwriting of Benedict Arnold, an American major-general in command at West Point, the matter smelled rankly of treason.

Washington was returning from Hartford to headquarters when he was diverted to West Point. An unexplainable bit of stupidity had allowed Arnold to learn of André's capture, and when Washington arrived at Arnold's headquarters opposite West Point he found the traitor's young wife in a state of collapse and Arnold himself fled to the British frigate "Vulture," which was already dropping downstream out of range.

From the upper windows of the Livingston house, in Dobbs Ferry, you may look northwest over the roofs of the town where André and Arnold had secretly met and plotted to betray the United States. Across the river you may see the faint outlines of the village of Tappan, where André was held prisoner, and where George Washington shared his breakfast with the convicted spy. At the foot of the hill in Dobbs Ferry you may see the landing where a group of British dignitaries came to plead with General Green for André's life. If you had been in Tappan the next morning you might have seen André walk to the gibbet, adjust the noose firmly about his own neck, and heard him say: "It will be but a momentary pang." With a record that included secret service during the siege of Charleston, André was undoubtedly a spy, but if you had watched dry-eyed as this man met death you would have been lonesome, for there were plenty of honest tears from the American officers who stood by and saw him hang.

With the plot exploded, Arnold a turncoat, André dead, the cause at least was safe. "Whom can we trust now?" asked Washington, and proceeded to find out. In spite of a wide-spread feeling of contempt for Arnold, his desertion made an impression upon the faint-hearts in both armies. In an effort to stiffen the morale of his men, and somewhat stung by the vengefulness of Arnold's threat in a letter presented at the Dobbs Ferry conference that he would make reprisals if André was killed, Washington conceived the idea of kidnapping Arnold in New York. The sergeant-major detailed for this bold stroke had the worst possible luck, missed Arnold by a half-hour, and landed on board a transport filled with a corps of deserters, bound for Virginia, and commanded by the traitor himself.

By June of 1781 the French army was ready for action. They marched across Connecticut, and pitched their tents upon the Westchester hills. That lively, attractive young aide-de-camp who danced with the girls of Westchester was a chap named Berthier, destined to become field marshal under Napoleon and Prince of Wagram; the tall, gallant Saxon aide was the Count de Fersen, later commander of the Swiss body-guard of Louis XVI. Custine commanded the Saintonge regiment—Custine who had served under Frederick the Great; on the ridge east of the Nepperhan were the Viomênil brothers—Count and Baron, soldiers both; over on the hill above White Plains was the charming Lauzun—he was guillotined a few years later. "Gentleman rankers out on a spree," and leading as gay an army of crimson- and white- and pink- and yellow- and blue- and green-clad troops as Europe could put in the field. What shortcomings they found with the entertainment their American allies offered, what irritation they felt at being served beef, potatoes, lamb and chicken on one plate, they forgot in the real comradeship that sprang up. New days were coming. New York, the stronghold, was to be beaten down by these keen French, and these dogged Americans, and Henry Clinton might well beware.

Washington moved his headquarters into the Livingston house at Dobbs Ferry. There on July 6, 1781 Rochambeau met and joined him and for the first time the armies were formally allied. The two commanders sat late over the plans for the effort which was presently to make Henry Clinton shout to Cornwallis and Tarleton for help. In the back of Washington's mind was a shrewd manoeuvre, and he kept it in the back of his mind, for if a plan was to be good enough to fool the enemy, it should be good enough to deceive his own men. Clinton was to be thoroughly scared by a demonstration by the combined armies against New York. If he called for reinforcements from the south, good; if they came, better yet. For it was not Clinton in New York whom Washington wanted, nor Tarleton in Charleston, but Cornwallis at Yorktown, the link between the two. And Washington knew that this was to be his last gamble with fate.

On July 18 Rochambeau accompanied him on a reconnoissance of the enemy's positions north of New York. What they saw led them to throw a protective cordon of troops across the peninsula of Westchester, from the Sound to the Hudson, to keep the British patrols from leaking out. Ten days later Washington heard that three British regiments from South Carolina had been sent to Clinton's relief. Back of his calm eyes his brain was humming with excitement. He wrote letters about his plans for attacking New York and then saw to it that those letters fell into the enemy's hands. When the British approached the American lines they found them preparing for battle. Washington allowed his engineers to survey camp sites and build brick ovens within sight of the enemy's scouts. And then, on August 3, a travel-worn messenger arrived with a letter from Lafayette.

"DeGrasse is sailing with the French fleet from Santo Domingo for Chesapeake Bay" was its message. The moment had come.

To the Livingston house he summoned Robert Morris, who had never failed before, and who must not fail now; and with him Richard Peters, the acting Secretary of State. Washington demanded men. Turning to Peters, he asked: "What can you do?"

"With money, everything. Without it, nothing," replied the

Secretary of State, and looked questioningly toward Morris. The banker produced a loan of $30,000. To Washington it was as good at that moment as a million, for it meant pay and food for his men, a promise of more men, and supplies for a forced march. And the forced march was imminent. Rochambeau came down from his headquarters up over the hill and the two laid their plans. On the eleventh 3000 Hessians from Cornwallis' forces arrived to defend New York. On August 25 all but 3000 men of the entire American army and the whole French force crossed the Hudson and were half-way to Philadelphia before Sir Henry Clinton knew that he had been tricked.

Two months later Cornwallis surrendered to the Allied armies, and there was no more British army between New York and Charleston. The plan which first saw daylight in the Livingston House at Dobbs Ferry ended the Revolution.

It was poetic justice, therefore, that in this house eighteen months later should occur the formal evacuation of the United States by the British. On the afternoon of May 6, 1783, two barges landed at the Ferry. In one was George Washington, Commander-in-Chief; in the other Governor Clinton of New York State. Presently a sloop-of-war appeared, and from it landed General Sir Guy Carleton, Commander-in-Chief of the British Expeditionary Forces. The three men met in the front room of the Livingston House, and at a sturdy round walnut table which stands in the house today General Sir Guy Carleton signed on the dotted line, renouncing a claim upon America which was first staked out by Sir Walter Raleigh. Good Queen Bess would have sworn like a lady at the spectacle; Guy Carleton, instead, marched out between four companies of American infantry at present-arms, saluted the flag, invited General Washington and Governor Clinton to dine aboard his sloop, and after an exceedingly

THE KENDALL HOUSE

good dinner fired a seventeen-gun salute for the guest who throughout the war had been scornfully referred to by Parliament as "Geo. Washington, Esqre."

From Philip Livingston, its Revolutionary occupant, the house passed into the hands of Peter Van Brugh Livingston, a rich, righteous and rigid citizen who was a member of two legislatures, and who acquired most of the real estate in Dobbs Ferry. A small parcel of this real estate he gave to the Episcopal Church. When a local tavern-keeper applied for admission to the church Van Brugh Livingston's influence and indignant protests almost kept the boniface out of reach of salvation. The house was purchased from Livingston by Stephen Archer, a gentle Quaker. His wife at her death-bed promised him that if he would build a bay window in the house and sit at that window on a Friday night, she would return to him. He built the bay window and every Friday night for twenty years sat peering out, straining his eyes to distinguish her ghostly form from the shadows of the ancient horse-chestnut tree. This is a true story of spiritualism: *she never came back*. Stephen Archer's daughter married a Dr. Hasbrouck and the house became his property upon her death. His fourth wife succeeded in outliving him, and in the light of Van Brugh Livingston's prejudice against tavern-keepers, it is interesting to recall the latest episode in the possession of the ancient dwelling.

Messmore Kendall, a lawyer of New York, was driving down Broadway one morning when he saw a sign in the dooryard of the Hasbrouck house advertising it for sale. He stopped. Inquiry from a woman who answered his knock brought out the information that financial stress had forced the sale of the house to a brewer who proposed to open a road house within its sacred walls. Mr. Kendall went on to the city. He learned from the real-estate brokers that the title was to be transferred to the brewer at 12 o'clock of the following day. At 12 o'clock there was no brewer in sight. At 1 o'clock Mr. Kendall had bought the house. At 5 o'clock of the same afternoon the brewer appeared, but the house had been saved forever.

So, instead of the clash of weapons of a dance orchestra, the Livingston House today hears the call of the birds from the garden. Instead of a coat of scarlet paint, a swinging tavern-sign, and the installation of new "service facilities" the house has undergone a complete restoration to its early beauty.

Where a less knowing eye would have altered for the sake of altering, he has directed changes only as they would preserve the feeling of self-effacing Colonial occupancy. Where the austerity of the period might easily have been made inelastic, he has made you sense the vital nearness of the glorious immortals who were there. Where the old frame of the building settled back after a century of service and gave an informal tilt to the door-frames, instead of replacing them with new he has tailored the old doors a trifle. He has left the old floors, for flooring such as men laid in those days was not to be disciplined for little irregularities. Between the drawing room and the study hangs the original front door, with a lock three hands broad, and the great key that turned on the invader's last good-bye. Even electricity came into the house in a quiet disguise. If it is candle-light, and you should peer into the low-studded dining-room, with its musket and pewter, and its great fireplace, you will be forgiven if your fancy pictures a Continental cavalryman bolting his supper at the end of the long table. Perfectly sane people have heard Lafayette's light step on the stair.

Given far less to work with than the Jumel Mansion a few miles away, the restorer of the Livingston house has avoided the error of formalizing the restoration. For years he had been collecting rare furniture for just such an emergency. Out of the storage warehouse and into the drawing room came a pair of sofas and a little table from the shop of Duncan Phyfe; two of Thomas Chippendale's mirrors; a pair of girandoles of unusual grace; a very early and tinkly American piano; and a dozen other things, each wearing a veil of antiquity over her charms. Like a group of delightful reunited old ladies they fell to chirruping and whispering, agreeing that this was *so* like home, when one—and it was probably one of the mischievous girandoles, who give back your reflection askew—suggested with a sparkle in her eyes: "Let's pretend we have always been here!" A whisper of assent fled from one to another. The Dutch clock in the hallway chimed agreement, the Queen Anne sofa on the landing heard and sighed happily, and one of Washington's own chairs in the study, which had left Mount Vernon a century ago, remarked that he had always regarded Dobbs Ferry as a comfortable asylum.

They will hush their chatter when you come in, and you cannot surprise them at it. But on a June night you may sit outside and watch the moon rise through the tracery of an old wistaria on the south portico. Listen sharply: when a white parrokeet waddles in from the blue shadows of the garden, and a voice is singing, and there is the lightest feather of air moving, it will bring their whisper through the window to you. The illusion is yours; they are at home, among their own.

THE LONGFELLOW HOUSE

THE LONGFELLOW HOUSE

It has the requisite dignity of its poet and its general, the well-dressed air of its Tory merchant, the scholarly simplicity of its lexicographer, the open-armed hospitality of its rich apothecary-general, and the grace of the lady who is its present châtelaine.

THE LONGFELLOW HOUSE

"THE moonlight poet," a clever Frenchman called him, "having little passion, but a calmness of attitude which approaches majesty." In a single deft pass of verbal legerdemain he conjures about the venerable head of Longfellow all the cool alluring mystery that veils a far-away mountain peak at night. He waves the magic word "moonlight" and the sun puffs out. In one stroke he has drawn a caricature which is not a character. The brightness of words tempted him into an error of drawing at which he would have paused if he had visited the poet's house.

For it is a yellow citadel stormed by sunlight from morning to night—sunlight pouring down upon its southerly wall and dancing off the terrace to ripple over the lawn, splashing in minor torrents through the tall windows of Martha Washington's room, and of the poet's red-curtained study opposite, slanting its mellow shafts at acute angles into the rooms on the north side, and breaking up at last into a carnival of color in the garden.

No such crisp epigram as the Frenchman's will dismiss the house. True, he would have found himself at home in the midst of gay colorings and an orderly clutter of interesting and precious garnitures, furniture, books and *objets d'art*. But as his critical faculties were trained upon the interior, as he began to retrace the history of this building, obviously so colonially American, and yet become so definitely of another period without losing its colonial flavor, he would have groped in vain for a bright phrase to polish off his impression.

The Longfellow house is "typical" of nothing, and we may thank heaven for that. It borrows here and there from architectural convention, improves vastly upon it here and there, accepts easily the change in fortunes, in family and in comforts of its successive owners. It has the requisite dignity of its poet and its general, the well-dressed air of its Tory merchant, the scholarly simplicity of its lexicographer, the open-armed hospitality of its rich apothecary-general, and the grace of the lady who is its present occupant. The composite of these qualities is a picture which is almost as familiar and as dear to America as Mount Vernon.

Out of that picture troops a story more varied in human incident than that of Washington's own home. It begins in 1759, when a Colonel Vassall built a splendid new house on Tory Row, the vulgar name for the *Via Sacra* of Cambridge, now called Brattle Street. Within a radius of a quarter-mile one might take tea with the Lees, dine with the last of the King's foresters, discuss politics with Richard Lechmere, or theology with the Reverend East Apthorp, without canvassing more than a small group of the sociable colony of royalists whose residences gave the street its nickname. Administrations change, the Tory "keynote" is perennial, and if your visit to Cambridge had been timed in the early seventies of the Eighteenth Century, the chances are that the prevailing topic of conversation in Tory Row would have been politics, and the keynote would have been—as today—"What are we coming to?"

At that particular season they came to an April forenoon of '75. A line of red-coats marched out from Boston at the double, past the college, and on into the country toward Lexington, where there was trouble. A few hours later they returned, also at the double, because there had been trouble in the country. On the tail of the British column came the men of Acton and Billerica and Carlisle and Concord, and of every village along the line of pursuit. Four civilians were killed at the corner of Dunster and Winthrop Streets—perhaps because they tried to oppose with well-aimed half-bricks the further retreat of a much-irritated British soldiery. The air of Cambridge became suddenly unhealthy for royalists, and darkness in the fine houses on Tory Row told its own story of the hurried departure of their owners.

The Vassalls fled to Halifax. Cambridge was becoming an armed camp, with incoming militia quartered where they saw fit to alight. The men of Marblehead made themselves very comfortable on the Vassall estate. The battle of Bunker Hill on June 17th, with heavy loss and no tangible advantage to either side, threw the camp into utter confusion and swelled the number of volunteers to fourteen thousand. They swarmed down in a great semicircle to sever the Boston peninsula from the mainland, while the British retired into the city to await reinforcements. Congress met, chose as commander of the army a young soldier-farmer from Virginia who had shown great intelligence in discussing military plans, and on July 3d he rode down Tory Row from Watertown, made one of the shortest public speeches on record, and took command of his army.

After a fortnight in the residence on Harvard Square, now known as Wadsworth House, he ordered the men of Marblehead out of the Vassall house to make room for his staff and headquarters. For ten months it was his base of operations, the longest period during which he occupied any headquarters during the Revolution. He came there the authorized commander of an undisciplined, inexperienced mob.

He left only after he had transformed that mob into an army, fed it, clothed it, armed it, guarded it from smallpox, and finally, with its valor and enthusiasm and skill, ejected the British from Boston for a more hospitable battleground to the southward.

The southeast room was his office. One day in the early winter of '75-6 an out-rider came in with good news, and presently Martha Washington "arrived in great ceremony, with a coach and four black horses, with postilions and servants in scarlet livery." She was installed in the sunny room across the hallway, the room from whose walls look down today the interesting faces of Sir William Pepperrell's children, and the same room in which you may find an exquisite onyx and metal goblet from the studio of that delightful international scamp, Benvenuto Cellini.

As chatelaine of headquarters she presided over a modest celebration of their wedding anniversary, although, Miss Alice Longfellow says, "the General had to be much persuaded by his aides." And there was a "Twelfth Night party" which is a tradition in the Longfellow family. On rare occasions since it has been repeated, once by a group of youngsters of all ages who impersonated in costume the guests of Washington, and some of those latter-day guests were direct descendants of the earlier dignitaries. On another winter night the Longfellow children dressed in the characters of the successive occupants of the house, and the sword of General Craigie clanked about the boots of a certain Boston lawyer until, as he says "I was no longer Dana; I felt like a regular profiteer!"

For the end of the Revolution was the beginning of a large period of hospitality in the life of General Andrew Craigie. He had been apothecary-general to the Continental army, and in the light of the recent war, it must be evident that purveying to any victorious army

THE LONGFELLOW HOUSE

is profitable. The Vassall House, during the seventeen years after Washington's departure, had been occupied by two good patriots: Nathaniel Tracy, who gave a hundred ships to the government during the war, and Thomas Russel, the same who set Timothy Dexter an example for making a fortune. Then Andrew Craigie (General, if you like) bought the house, and it bears his name as commonly today as that of the poet.

Hawthorne, the quiet, handsome young writer who used to visit the house years later, should have known General Craigie. For all his garden parties at Commencement time, with their distinguished guests, like Talleyrand, and Admiral d'Estaing, and Prince Edward (the father of Queen Victoria), for all the refinishing and painting he did in the house, for all the splendor of the organ which he installed in the northeast room between two fine Corinthian columns, and the rare girandole in the study, and the Adam mantels—for all his creature magnificence, he had a scenario or two concealed about his person.

Hark!

"I am the ghost of Madame Craigie. I loved an impetuous youth from the south, then a student. We parted, for my family forbade me. But we swore to write each other. He did not write; I pined; then, desperate, obeyed my parents' mandates, and married General Craigie. And as we sat at table in his great house, a letter came to me, in my maiden name—the name, ah me! now forfeit—saying 'I have no word of you, no word since I went away. Why do you not write?' And *then* I knew that they had kept his letters from me, and mine from him! And from that day I never spoke to my husband save on matters of essential business."

Hawthorne could have made something out of that.

Or this: the poet was surprised one morning as he came downstairs to see lying on one of the lower treads a letter. It was a fervent letter, with no clue to the addressee nor to its source. Inquiry disclosed nothing from any member of the household. The next morning another letter—also fervent. When it happened again and still again, he set himself to solve the mystery. And it was no mystery, for in the Craigie dynasty there had been an affair, which Andrew was only too anxious not to pile on his wife's already considerable grievance. So he walled the letters up under the stairs, and thought them safe. But as the sea gives up her dead, the gradual settling of the staircase and the tapping of feet upon it slowly and inexorably provoked a crack through which revenge fed the letters, one by one, confiding the story piecemeal, to a poet.

Capricious investments sent Craigie to his grave in 1818 a poor man. If Madam Craigie was in the slightest degree relieved at his departure, her obligation to him was diluted by the fact that she must now support herself. By "taking in boarders" she could manage to live on in the old house, and make ends meet. For those who could pass her rather rigid inspection it offered accommodation far better than the average. Naturally such folk as Edward Everett and his bride, and President Jared Sparks of Harvard and Josiah Worcester, who wrote a dictionary, needed no references. With strangers it was different. A gentle young fellow with light hair and deep-set eyes, and a clean, aquiline profile, appeared one afternoon in 1837 and asked for lodgings. She said she had none vacant. In the temporizing dialogue which followed it developed that his name was Longfellow and that he was the author of a book she had quite recently been reading, and her manner thawed so readily that he got the room.

He was not much trouble, really—only a polite young man from Maine who had lost his wife a year or two before, and who had just been made professor of modern languages in the College. He was usually up in his room writing at night, while Mrs. Craigie read Voltaire or Madame de Sevigné down in the library, or played an old song on an old pianoforte. Another paying guest was a Miss Sally Lowell, whose talented nephew, James Russell Lowell, was beginning to be heard from; a third was the lexicographer Worcester, who was so taken with the house that he later bought it. For Longfellow's part, they were amiable neighbors, but not so exacting as to interrupt the absorbing routine of a man of thirty embarking upon a full professorship.

For nearly twenty years he served the College in this capacity. The College was thrifty, and anxious to get the most out of his teaching; Longfellow's health was not good, and the duties of his position asked more of him than he could sometimes give. He had resolved as a youth to become an eminent man of letters, just as determinedly as any man in business ever set his face toward the height of power. He kept a diary of progress, as scrupulous a record in its own line as the balance sheets of an industry, and he never allowed himself to be diverted by praise or ill-health from the pursuit of his ambition. Steadily and smoothly there came from his pen an output toward which the public looked with growing anticipation. Now it was experimental, now political, now religious. The best of it came from the warmest corner of a warm patriotic heart, where he kept a great treasure of the legends of his own country.

When *Hiawatha, Evangeline*, and *The Courtship of Miles Standish* had appeared, his fame had crossed boundaries and oceans. Word-mongers say they are not his finest work, but they went straight from his heart to the heart of plain people everywhere. His enthusiasm for the Indian tradition that is our only native folklore found utterance in *Hiawatha;* the story of Evangeline he got from Hawthorne; the romance of John Alden and Priscilla Mullins he picked from his own family tree. As a poet he gave the lie to the precious though fashionable complaint that nothing real in art need be expected from America until she had had a century or two of sandpapering. His enthusiasm of race drew occasional outbursts of a greater quality —the thing that made him a great citizen as well as a great national artist—the immortal spirit which went into such majestic songs as *The Building of the Ship.* "In neither case," observes Higginson, "was this Americanism trivial, wasteful, or ignoble in its tone." Will the professional hucksters of 100-per-centism please copy?

Contrary to persistent tradition, a poet is not a sulky hermit plucking ideas from empty air and full bottles. Longfellow had about him a laboratory full of elixirs of association, to which his sensitive spirit was a quick reagent. His second marriage gave him a beloved wife, his wife's father gave Mrs. Longfellow the Craigie house to live in always, and Mrs. Longfellow gave her husband the children who were the Alpha and Omega of his affection for children in general. The familiar portrait of the children hangs in the dining-room; a pretty picture, painted by Reed, the same who wrote "Sheridan's Ride."

Harvard activities supplied him with a circle of friends which spread like ripples in a pond with every new literary production he cast forth. Come into his study and meet the best of them. A fine white room on the front of the house, high ceiling, tall windows, bright turkey-red curtains falling from borders scalloped like a flounce from Godey's *Ladies' Book.* An orange-tree flourishing in a tub at a sunny window—as it was when he stood at his high desk and wrote of Spain. Most of his writing was done at a round Duncan Phyfe table, whose graces are hidden under a faded green felt cover. On its dusty self-pattern of ivy leaves are the articles he left there as he died: *item*, a miscellany of books; *item*, an ornate ink-well of Coleridge which Longfellow treasured; *item*, a historic ink-well which had been the successive property of Moore and Crabbe, which Longfellow venerated; and, *item*, a little tupenny glass ink-bottle which Longfellow himself used! Even the quill pens are there with which he formed that calm, round graceful handwriting.

You came to see his friends. You shall. Here is a spare young man with a sensitive, kindly smile about the eyes—from Concord he is, and his name is Emerson. Over in that extraordinarily long armchair by the hearth sits (on his shoulder-blades) a handsome chap, the only man who fits the chair—six feet and more of Charles Sumner. On the walls are the crayon portraits customary as gifts before the days of the camera: here is Felton, whom Dickens called "the heartiest of Greek professors"; here that fascinating Agassiz, always shuttling between Cambridge and some tropic or other; here Hawthorne's grave dark eyes.

Picture him later in life chatting before the fire with Lowell, Holmes, John Lothrop Motley, or Whittier. Shift the scene to a Boston tavern with the same company, and three or four more of their stature, engaged in starting *The Atlantic Monthly*, and ask yourself where a poet could seek more inspiration. Gossips who knew this group only from outside called it the "Mutual Admiration Society," and you may find in the Boston Athenaeum a review of *Evangeline* written by Felton on which some scoffing contemporary has pencilled "*Insured at the Mutual.*" There is good authority for picturing Longfellow and a pair of younger cronies returning under the moon from a good dinner at Porter's, singing in harmony—"I am a Rajah!! Putterum!" And in the years when the Saturday

Club was flourishing, the poet was a regular attendant, and a modest, dry-spoken commentator on discussions in which the Olympians matched wits.

Every eminent visitor to Boston paid him court and even Oscar Wilde paid him a patronizing call. Many came who were not eminent, and the poet often invited aimless tourists in to see the house. To one such couple he exhibited the Coleridge ink-well, explaining helpfully that Coleridge had written *The Ancient Mariner.* "Oh," said the bridegroom, and nodded. Then, puzzled, he said: "Say! who done the *Old Oaken Bucket?*" There were memorable evenings spent in the Howe tavern at Sudbury with Ole Bull, the fiddler, and an ingenious group of story-tellers whose yarns took shape in "The Tales of a Wayside Inn."

Longfellow in his later years was the chief figure of Cambridge. Great men and women came to pay him tribute and to find his modesty unimpeached. When the undergraduates started a mutiny over in the College and riotous language was echoing from the red brick of old "Mass." hall, it was quieted when one youth cried: "Let's hear what Mr. Longfellow has to say about it—he's fair, at any rate." And when the spreading chestnut tree over Dexter Pratt's smithy fell, the children of Cambridge gave their pennies to fashion him an armchair of its wood, and used to traipse fearlessly into the Longfellow house from time to time to call on the poet and see that the chair gave him good service. Without question it is one of the homeliest chairs in the world—and one of the finest.

One cannot leave the house without a glance at his other friends, his closer intimates, nor enter the house without remarking them. Books, books, books—heavy Italian walnut cases of them, white shelves of them, heaps of them, in the study, the halls, the dining-

THE LONGFELLOW HOUSE

room, the drawing room, a vault full of the rarest of them in the east entry. I have not visited the pantry, but I will make a small wager that there are books on the cake-box. It is a judicious collection by a man who was a hungry reader and a lover of beautiful volumes. There are ranks of Italian folios, Tasso and Ariosto in white vellum —and of apparently everything else in equally rich costume, for the years of the poet's great public appreciation built for him a formidable library of handsomely bound presentation copies and he was no mean purchaser himself.

They are where the poet left them, and so they will stay. When the actual tenancy of the house by the Longfellow heirs comes to a period, it will be held securely in trust just as it is, just as he left it one March day in 1882. Those generous and tactful heirs have already given the city of Cambridge the park which affords the house a clear vista to the Charles, and have given Longfellow land across the Charles to make up most of Soldiers Field, the great playground of Harvard. Now they have wisely provided that the house shall not become a museum, but that it shall remain the home of whose atmosphere and influence they cherish so acute an appreciation.

Longfellow's bust stands in Westminster Abbey, the first American so to be honored. It is made of marble, and is a good likeness. Longfellow's soul lives in Cambridge, in his home. The house is a better likeness than the bust, and of warmer stuff. His children's trust will perpetuate their generosity for our children's children.

A dignified old clock stands on the stairs, and ticks:

"Forever—never
Never—forever."

CLIVEDEN

MONTICELLO

"Mr. Jefferson," said one of Rochambeau's aides, "is the first American who has consulted the fine arts to know how he should shelter himself from the weather." With no continental travel for background, with only the meager pictorial record of the period to draw upon, he somehow responded instantly to the simplicity and useful beauty of the classics, and translated it to his castle.

CLIVEDEN

One of Maxwell's six-pounders spoke, and a ball passed in the front window of the Chew house, through four partitions and heaven knows how many British, and out a rear window. The battery hammered at the steps, the windows and the door, while snipers fired at the flash of a rifle from the upper stories. Infantry charged across the lawn and was beaten back, artillery punctured but did not dislodge. Reed was all for chasing the rest of the retreating British toward the city, but Knox said it was against the rules to leave an enemy fort in the rear. "What!" Reed exclaimed, "Call this a fort and lose the happy moment?"

CLIVEDEN

A DAUGHTER of the Quincy house saw the beginning of the Revolution. Mount Vernon was the home of its chief figure. From the Jumel Mansion he retreated to Westchester when the Continental army suffered its first major reverse. In the Kendall house at Dobbs Ferry he conceived the campaign which was to end the war, and there finally he saw the British evacuate the United States. Five houses in America punctuate the Revolutionary career of Washington, and the fifth is the house where the cause of freedom entered the dark hours, the period of terrible ordeal.

Cliveden was built in 1761 on "the worst road in America," the main street of Germantown. The village, whose houses dotted some three miles of the street, was already becoming a fashionable summer retreat for prominent Philadelphians, and William Chew, the attorney general of the province, made Cliveden large enough for a family that totalled fourteen children, with the appropriate retinue of servants and household pets. The house is three stories high, as severely rectangular as a mill, with a plain extension built to the rear, and a further detached addition connected only by an underground passage. It might easily have been commonplace, but the dapple-gray native stone of which it is built is interesting, the doorway, to which you ascend by a flight of six stone steps, is dignified and inviting, and dormer windows, fat chimneys, and stone urns strike notes of real character on an otherwise plain roof. It makes no great bid for beauty, but its aspect of substance is as honest as a Philadelphia lawyer—and that is what William Chew was.

Although he became chief justice of Pennsylvania under the crown, he was no more of a loyalist than his position required. As a model of astute straddling, where can you cite a statement which quite compares with his decision, rendered in answer to the question: What is to become of those who meet the mandates of the crown with armed resistance?

"I have stated," he answered, "that an opposition by force of arms to the lawful authority of the King or his Ministry is high treason, but in the moment when the King or his Ministers shall exceed the authority vested in them by the Constitution submission to their mandate becomes treason." The same tolerance he showed toward the uprising of the colonies he showed to their leaders in Philadelphia, and you may take it from John Adams' diary that he was a rare and upright judge of food as well as of treason.

"Thursday. Dined with Mr. Chew, Chief Justice of the Province, with all the gentlemen from Virginia . . . and many others. About four o'clock we were called down to dinner. The furniture was all rich. Turtle and every other thing, flummery, jellies, sweetmeats, of 20 sorts, trifles, whipped sillabubs, floating islands, fools, etc., and then a dessert of fruits, raisens, almonds, pears, peaches, wines most excellent & admirable. I drank Madeira at a great rate & found no inconvenience in it."

However much the members of the Continental Congress enjoyed his hospitality in 1775, they could no longer endure his presence as chief justice in Philadelphia in 1777, and in August of that year he and Governor John Penn were arrested and escorted to Burlington, New Jersey. Within a month Washington had met the British in

CLIVEDEN

force at the Brandywine in a doubtful effort to check their march on Philadelphia, and had been defeated. For a fortnight he played hide-and-seek with Howe on the banks of the Schuylkill, and if the countryside had been as communicative to him as it was to the enemy, the enemy would not have marched, as he presently did, unmolested into Philadelphia. Howe placed his major force at Germantown, and Washington came in as near as he dared and sat down to watch and wait. Strategically, the Revolution was a distinctly suburban war. With Philadelphia, the national capital, in the hands of the British, and winter coming on, American morale was quoted at .001, with no sales.

On the night of October 2–3, the American forces marched quietly down the main road toward Germantown, with flanks thrown out, on the right to the Wissahickon ravine, on the left to the old York pike. Dawn brought Sullivan of Maine into contact with the enemy. The enemy retreated, gaining speed as he scampered down Mount Airy into Germantown, with Sullivan, Conway and Reed at his heels. Colonel Musgrave, of the Fortieth Regiment of the British, saw the retreat coming, and with one hundred and twenty men swarmed into Cliveden, closed the shutters on the lower floor, barred the doors, and prepared to stand. Washington himself was in the pursuit, and he ordered Maxwell and four cannon to the ground across the street from Cliveden, where Upsala now stands. A thick fog had gathered, making it nearly impossible to determine where the enemy was, or in what strength. The utmost confusion prevailed. One of Maxwell's six-pounders spoke, and a ball passed in the front window of the Chew house, through four partitions and heaven knows how many British, and out a rear window. The battery hammered at the steps, the windows and the door, while snipers fired at the flash of rifles from the upper stories. Infantry charged across the lawn and were beaten back, artillery punctured, but did not dislodge. Reed was all for chasing the rest of the retreating British toward the city, but Knox said it was against the rules to leave an enemy fort in the rear. "What!" Reed exclaimed, "call this a fort and lose the happy moment?"

It was in effect a fort, but it was as truly the happy moment to leave the fort to be cleaned out later and press the British retreat. For the American wings had not driven the British back (the American left wing failed because General Stephen was drunk), and the British, unopposed, marched obliquely toward the center of the fighting at Cliveden. Thus the battle became, instead of the conflict of bow-shaped forces, the meeting of two great arrowheads, and the point where the arrows met and the sparks were flying thickest was the lawn of the Chew house. Smith of Virginia, a colonel, set out for the house with a flag of truce to demand Musgrave's surrender, and was shot from a window. Major White, one of Sullivan's aides, tried to set fire to the house, and a shot from a cellar window killed him. Musgrave hung on. Every minute that passed brought British troops nearer, and increased the odds against the Americans.

Our army left five hundred dead and wounded in Germantown and then retreated to Whitemarsh. The King's forces, reduced by five hundred dead and wounded, remained in the bloody fog of the village. The townsfolk began to come out of their cellars and examine the damage. A field hospital was set up at Wyck, a fine old house down Germantown Road. At Johnson House you can see today the hole in a window-frame through which a frantic pet squirrel, forgotten in the flight to the cellar, gnawed his way to freedom. Stray bullets pierced every house within a quarter-mile, and of all the houses within that radius, Cliveden, its center, took the worst punishment.

CLIVEDEN

Five carpenters worked all that fall and winter repairing the damage. Holes gaped through the inner walls, hardly a pane of glass was intact, statues were chipped, mirrors splintered, furniture reduced to expensive kindling. What was not stained with blood was streaked with smoke, and the second floor ceilings were sprayed with bullets by Continentals who dashed into the shelter of the building and fired through the upper windows.

Across the span of the years we can still hear the echo of an outraged protest—the hymn of hate of the daughters of William Chew, sung with all the cordial detestation that could be uttered by a group of sisters who came out to Germantown under British escort and found their lovely home in ruins at the hands of the army that had already made their father a prisoner. None can blame them for the gayety with which they entered into the social life of that winter in the occupied city, with never a thought for Washington's men shivering in the snow at Valley Forge. Knyphausen, Cornwallis, and the two Howes picked out comfortable quarters in the deserted houses of the patriots who had fled, and Major André settled down with a "rapacious crew" in the home of Benjamin Franklin. When Franklin's daughter returned after the British evacuation the next June she reported to him in Paris: "They stole and carried off with them some of your musical instruments, viz., a Welsh harp, ball harp, the set of tuned bells which were in a box, viol-de-gamba, all the spare harmonica glasses and one or two spare cases." Tuneful was the life of the army of occupation.

André was paying diligent court to Peggy Chew. He was her champion in the fête of Mischianza, and her gallant protector when a marauding force of ragged Continentals marched down from Valley Forge and broke up the party. He wore her ribbon. with the legend

"No Rival," presented her with an aquarelle of himself in costume, wrote an account of the affair in verse, and filled in his spare hours by inditing to her rhapsodies inspired in the orchard at Cliveden, in apple-blossom time. Then came the parting; within a few short years

> "The youth who bids with stifled pain
> His sad farewell tonight"

was dead with a rope around his neck, and although Peggy married a soldier of the Republic, she remembered the enemy gallant. She was never so impishly amused as when she could say a kind word for André, for it guaranteed an explosive protest from her husband. "Major André," said Peggy, demurely, with a certain dangerous sadness in her eyes, "was a most witty and cultivated gentleman," and Colonel Howard, seizing a visitor's arm, exclaimed "He was a damned spy, sir! Nothing but a damned spy!"

The house had been restored only two years when William Chew sold it to Blair McClenahan, but in 1787 he bought it back. In August of 1787 Washington, then president of the Constitutional Convention, rode out to see the encampment at Whitemarsh to which he had retreated ten years before, and dined with McClenahan in the Chew house. Despite his Royalist relations, the close of the Revolution restored Benjamin Chew to good standing in his community and the judicial profession, and he served as justice of the High Court of Errours and Appeals until its abolishment in 1808. During the period when the Federal Congress sat in Philadelphia it was no infrequent thing to see the Father of His Country in company with the father of Peggy and of Harriet, who was soon to marry a Carroll of Doughoregan.

It was at Germantown that Stephen's drunkenness left his divi-

CLIVEDEN

sion without a commander, and opened a vacancy for Lafayette's assumption of an active command as major-general. Naturally, therefore, when Lafayette returned to America in 1825, he could not ignore Germantown. He was received with a military escort and drawn "in an open barouche" to Cliveden. Let Miss Ann Johnson, of Upsala, across the way, carry on the story as she did in a letter to her mother:

"Last 4th. day morn I had the honour of breakfasting with Lafayette at Mr. Chew's. I wish you had been here—the house both up and down stairs was crowded with men, women and soldiers—and around the house. Mrs. and two of the Miss Morris's and myself were the only invited ladies that sat down to Breakfast—about 16 sat down at first, and when they had finished others took their place, and so on till I believe nearly all the soldiers had breakfast—those that did not come in had something in the kitchen. I heard that they eat everything they had till at last the cook had to lock the doors.

"I was introduced to LaFayette twice and shook hands with him three times. Ann Chew regretted M. was not there to enjoy the scene—it was quite delightful to see anything so animated in G—pp. There was so much noise that I could not hear a word the General said; every person seemed so anxious to see him eat that a centinal had to keep guard at the door with a drawn sword—it was very fine indeed. When he departed the shouts of the multitude and the roaring of the cannon was almost deafening. A. L. Logan said I could give you a very fine description of it—but I told him I would have to leave it to your imagination, it would be impossible for me to describe everything."

Mrs. Samuel Chew is the present owner of the estate, and an

appreciative custodian of its legend. Hers are the Washington letters; the portraits of illustrious Chews who have been eminent in the law, medicine, and public affairs since John Chew sailed into Jamestown in the *Charitie* in 1621; the shot-holes, the stains of the powder-kegs on the floor; the immaculately carved columns and stair rail of the hallway, and the hundred other fragments of the Cliveden story. Cliveden is hers—its story is the nation's.

THE WENTWORTH MANSION

THE WENTWORTH MANSION

I like to think of the house as a family group of all the *Wentworths*, each little excrescence on the original nucleus being one of the useful but obscure members posed kneeling or sitting on the outskirts of the family as it pyramids up to the bulk of the council-room Benning Wentworth built, the council-room being in my mind's eye none other than the formidable, homely, well-fed and hard-drinking Benning himself.

THE WENTWORTH MANSION

> "These tales you tell are one and all
>   Of the Old World," the Poet said,
> "Flowers gathered from a crumbling wall,
>   Dead leaves that rustle as they fall;
>   Let me present you in their stead
> Something of our New England earth, . . ."
> 			—*Lady Wentworth.*

IT was almost as original in Colonial New Hampshire to be a Wentworth as it is today to be a Biddle in Philadelphia. The descendants of Samuel Wentworth, the first of his name in the province, were conspicuously numerous in the small population of their community. As individuals they were energetic, persevering, and not without a certain amount of dignity. To say that they were politicians is to say that they were business men. Individually they were better than average citizens, collectively they contributed enough to the progress and the story of New Hampshire to invite a glimpse into the house which is today the chief memorial to the family.

Except for its size you might pass it by in a countryside full of rambling buildings silvered by the weather. It has neither the warm, open-armed welcome of Doughoregan Manor, nor the smug comfort of Cliveden, nor the exalted location of Monticello, nor the decorative dignity of its rival, the Pepperrell House across the harbor. A plain man built it somewhere back in the seventeenth century, built it close by the bright water of Little Harbor because there were codfish there as sacred to New Hampshire revenue as any goldfish that ever inspired faith in Massachusetts. Built it out of big timber to cut the northeasters whipping in over the Isles of Shoals, built a sharp roof to shed snow. Built it to live in. Another generation, with perhaps a larger family, wanted more room, and built on. When Mark Hunking owned it he did the same. In the south our colonies' increased demands upon the facilities of a growing estate were met by outbuildings set well apart from the great house, but in this sharp climate outbuildings raised the unpleasant prospect of wading to and fro through shoulder-high drifts, and involved separate heating-plants and no end of inconvenience. So gradually the house sprouted a plain ell here and a humble jog there, a shed around the corner, and enough additions to effect a total of nearly fifty rooms. I like to think of the house as a family group of all the Wentworths, of each little addition to the original nucleus as one of the useful but obscure members posed kneeling or sitting on the outskirts of the family as it pyramids up to the great bulk of the council-room Benning Wentworth built, the council-room being in my mind's eye none other than the formidable, homely, well-fed and hard-drinking Benning himself.

To paint for yourself the picture of the prime of the house you must recall certain facts about the Portsmouth of the beginning of the eighteenth century. Twenty miles inland Indians scalped white men and women, and white men scalped Indians. As many miles to the eastward, and more, the men of Portsmouth sailed in ships for fish and returned with a catch to pay the storekeeper's bill for groceries and clothing—a bill which always seemed just out of reach, and which kept these men sailing until they died, while the merchants prospered. From the outer world came small-pox. Over on Great Island, at the Walton place, there were genuine witches; if you don't believe this you may read it in a pamphlet published in London in 1698, whose title says it is

> "an Exact and True Account of the various actions of infernal Spirits, or (*Devils Incarnate*) Witches, or both; and the great Disturbance and Amazement they gave to *George Walton's* Family at a place called *Great Island* in the Province of *New Hampshire* in New England, chiefly in throwing about (by an Invisible hand) *Stones*, *Bricks*, and *Brick-bats* of all sizes, with several other things, as *Hammers*, *Mauls*, *Iron-Crows*, *Spits*, and other domestick utensils, as came into their Hellish Minds, and this for the space of a Quarter of a Year."

The Province, though a royal property as distinguished from a chartered colonial settlement, was not encouraging to the farmer, not ready for the miller. Its governorship was for the king's favorite candidate, and in size and importance it was a homely stepsister of the well-to-do colony of Massachusetts to the southward.

John Wentworth bought the lieutenant-governorship and made it profitable until he died. From his widow, Mark Hunking's daughter, Benning Wentworth inherited the Mansion at Little Harbor. As a young graduate of Harvard who had brought home a Boston bride, and as the owner of a prosperous business and a fine house, he was popular enough, and his path was paved into politics. The Assembly applauded his protests against the Governor of Massachusetts who also governed New Hampshire. As a member of the council his youthful oratory soon moderated to the whisper of the boss who is learning how to do things smoothly, for there was much to be gained if London could be persuaded to appoint a distinct governor for New Hampshire who would not be responsible to Massachusetts. In 1744 the opportunity came to prove his point.

Benning Wentworth sold a cargo of lumber to an agent of the

King of Spain. When it reached Cadiz the agent had resigned, and his successor refused the cargo. On the return voyage the ship foundered, and Wentworth and a handful of sailors counted themselves lucky to be rescued. He went at once to London to beg the government to enforce his claim on Spain. With similar complaints from other British merchants a bill was presented at Madrid which Spain honored but did not pay, and under economic pressure England declared war upon her. At home, meanwhile, Governor Belcher had fallen into every trap his enemies set for him, and was removed, but not before the King had been prevailed upon to separate Massachusetts and New Hampshire once and for all, re-survey their boundaries, and set up a new governor not only in Boston but in Portsmouth.

Theoretically, John Thomlinson, the agent of New Hampshire in London, brought this about, but, as a matter of fact, it was Thomlinson's good aim and Benning Wentworth's timely cartridges which shot Governor Belcher's support from under him. What more natural, therefore, than that Benning Wentworth return to Portsmouth as governor of New Hampshire. He was received with cheers, and made a hearty address to his Assembly, suggesting that they make him a guaranteed annual grant of salary. The Assembly replied with fulsome cordiality and said they would grant him whatever they found themselves able to pay. It proved to be £500 a year, and to this Thomlinson presently managed to add the job of Surveyor of the Woods, which he bought from the previous surveyor for two thousand pounds and turned over to Wentworth for a consideration not mentioned. In order to accept the post the Governor had to surrender his claims for $56,000 against the Court of Spain, and the prospects were so bright in his new position that he was glad enough to do it in favor of additional income of £800, and to settle down to a smooth program of political patronage.

It happened that he was not to be allowed to forget the Court of Spain, nor to get rich without making enemies. England's war with Spain dragged France in, and Governor Shirley of Massachusetts, full of enthusiasm for his new charge, looked on a map for the nearest French stronghold, found it to be Louisburg, on Cape Breton Island, and shouted for money, arms, and men for an expedition. Benning Wentworth, who liked Shirley and often asked his advice, heard the cry, and offered New Hampshire help. Shirley took the help, and appointed a rival merchant in Portsmouth, William Pepperrell, as general in command.

Here was a delicate situation. Shirley, having securely appointed Pepperrell, wrote: "It would have been an infinite satisfaction to me, and done great honor to the expedition if your limbs would have permitted you to take the command." Wentworth was so charmed with the idea that he forgot his gout and volunteered! To this Shirley replied, with more truth than tact, that "any alteration of the present command would be attended with great risque, both with respect to the Assembly and the soldiers being entirely disgusted." "You was made General," wrote a friend to Pepperrell, "being a popular man, most likely to raise soldiers soonest. The expedition was calculated to ESTABLISH Shirley and make his creature Wentworth Governor of Cape Breton, which is to be a place of refuge for him from his creditors. Beware of snakes in the grass and mind their hissing." About four thousand men rallied, a fleet of a hundred vessels assembled, and the voyage began, planned by a Governor, and commanded by a merchant, to storm a citadel called the "Gibraltar of America."

Contemporaries called it a "Cambridge commencement," and

without a wild sort of undergraduate enthusiasm it must have failed. An enthusiastic preacher gave Governor Shirley a plan for investing the fortress which he had worked out himself. Another amateur gave him a model of a flying bridge to be used in scaling the walls—it only needed twelve hundred feet of rope to operate, and a thousand men might pass over it in four minutes. Shirley took his own counsel, drew his own beautifully-timed plans, and designed his own scaling ladders and pikes. The men were growing restless when George Whitefield, the eminent Newburyport counterpart of our own Billy Sunday, devised a motto "nihil desperandum Christo duce," and the expedition sailed like fanatic crusaders out of Boston Harbor, unscathed by a severe epidemic of small-pox in the port.

Every plan Shirley made went wrong. The fortress, instead of being surprised by the fleet, woke up the morning of April 29 to see it lying off the harbor. Yet on June 17 the well-scared commander of the citadel hauled down the French flag. The Yankees took the city, hauled the Tricolor up again, and lured several valuable prizes into port in this way. Pepperrell was made a Baronet, Commodore Warren an Admiral. England forced France to make peace, and gave Louisburg back. Do you, perhaps, see now why they called it a Cambridge commencement?

Governor Wentworth, though not a participant, shared vicariously in the glory of the expedition, and kept busy at home directing the fighting in the west against French Indians who raided the frontier stockades from the New York lakes. Gradually and thoroughly he installed his relatives in lucrative positions of the provincial government. An occasional quarrel with his Assembly brought forth a protest to the King to remove him and place Pepperrell in his stead. Unruffled, he would call his council to the mansion at Little Harbor,

THE WENTWORTH MANSION

set out an enormous punch-bowl on the council-room sideboard, and conduct the affairs of state as swiftly as a governor should who wants to move on to the card-rooms for a friendly game.

From his office above he could keep a weather eye on the ships out for the West Indies with lumber and livestock and fish and oil, and could tick off those inward-bound with molasses and coffee and rum. Toward town he could glimpse the stocks where more ships were building to tie his wilderness province, with its twenty miles of seacoast, to the outside world. If the Assembly lost its manners and had to be attended to, he stepped to the landing at the council-room door, and was royally wafted away to town in his official barge. His aims were not all selfish by any means. He gave a grant of land in the Connecticut valley on which to build Dartmouth College, he drew from the Assembly a grant of 300 pounds to restore a part of the burned library of Harvard. If his wife and his son had been spared to him, his life would have been very happy. But they were not spared, and thus innocently they contribute to the story of the house its most entertaining episode.

The kindly poet in the Craigie House told it in the *Tales of a Wayside Inn*. Shorn of its poetic embellishments, it is this: The Governor grew lonely in the great house. He had lost his wife, his boy, his figure. A maid of Portsmouth caught his eye, but she loved a sailor, and would have none of the Governor and his city ways. Accordingly, the sailor was caught by a press-gang and shipped to sea. Benning Wentworth grew lonelier, until one day he summoned to his house a number of guests, among them the Reverend Arthur Brown. After a good dinner he fixed a firm eye upon the dominie and said: "You are here, sir, to marry me." The company was astounded, and asked for the bride, whereupon the Governor turned and introduced as his blushing betrothed a maid-of-all-work in the house, Martha Hilton. And so, as so often happens, they were married.

> "The rector read the service loud and clear:
> 'Dearly beloved, we are gathered here,'
> And so on to the end. At his command
> On the fourth finger of her fair left hand
> The Governor placed the ring; and that was all:
> Martha was Lady Wentworth of the Hall!"

The son of the present owner of the house, Mr. J. Templeman Coolidge, tells me that marrying Martha did not necessarily indicate a loss of caste on the Governor's part, for it was customary in those days for girls of good families to work in the households of other good families. Further, there are none of the poet's "stacks of chimneys rising high in air," nor oaken panels and tapestries. Further still, it is doubtful whether Martha, as a barefoot child about the streets of Portsmouth, ever resolved that some day she would marry the

> ". . . portly person with three-cornered hat,
> A crimson velvet coat, head high in air,
> Gold-headed cane, and nicely powdered hair
> And diamond buckles sparkling at his knees,
> Dignified, stately, florid, much at ease."

But so many inaccurate legends have been edited to make dull facts that it is a real pleasure to concede the Hall to Martha, and Martha to her husband.

It was a fine house, there is no gainsaying that. Its fifty rooms must have pleased her, for they outranked in number any house in the whole countryside. There were queer proportions to them, and unexpected turns, one went up two steps into this room, and down three into that. A secret staircase led from the main portion of the house down to the water, which may have been built so that the Governor could escape an angry populace, or not, as you prefer. There was a big pantry to warm any woman's heart, and a still to make rum to warm any man's. It is a temptation to visualize the interior as filled with an oriental profusion of decorative objects, but the probability is that although Benning Wentworth had a florid taste for the creature comforts, and the ships handy to import them, he was still a native of New Hampshire and restrained in his notions of decoration. A guess—and it must be a guess, for no record exists—is that the house has much the same aspect today, with good portraits, like Copley's of Dorothy Quincy, good Windsor chairs, good Sheraton, good china, good wall-paper—and not too much of any ingredient to leave you surfeited. In the council-room we know that there was a heavily carved mantel which was strong and handsome, for it is so today; that the guns of the governor's guard were racked there, for they are there still; that there were paneled doors and wainscoating fit for a room in which to entertain Washington, as Martha Hilton Wentworth did entertain him here in 1789.

In 1766 Benning Wentworth resigned the governorship. He had seen the Stamp Act committed and repealed, and although he had treated with political daintiness the unpopular measures which were breeding trouble, he had held office longer than any other provincial governor, and had served his people in a way which encouraged their commercial growth. The office passed to his nephew, John Wentworth. In 1770 Benning Wentworth died, leaving Martha to marry Colonel Michael Wentworth, and a daughter, Martha, whom Governor John Wentworth married.

Five years later the storm broke at Lexington. The news sped to Portsmouth and every man armed himself and began drilling.

Governor John was powerless to resist the tendency. He tried to pack the Assembly with favorable delegates from new towns, and the Assembly angrily threw them out. When one of them insulted the Assembly, the Assembly chased him until, breathless, he slammed the three-inch door of the Wentworth mansion in their faces. The crowd brought a field-piece, pointed it at the door and demanded his surrender. He gave himself up, and the Governor, outraged at the affront, fled to the fort. His last official act was to prorogue the Assembly. Royal government in New Hampshire came to an end, and in John Wentworth the people lost a leader who had been energetic in the extension of learning, in the building of good roads, and in the development of agriculture. He lived on at Little Harbor until Martha Hilton died in 1805, and then went to England, and the house passed out of the family.

Its history for the past century has not been eventful. A critic who has traveled over certain of New Hampshire's roads may suggest that Governor John Wentworth was the last man who improved them, but that is neither here nor there, and such comment is only likely to call down upon the scoffer's head one of the ghosts without which no American colonial mansion is properly furnished. Jack Coolidge, as a boy, used to lie up in the loft and moan like a regulation ghost when disagreeable tourists asked to be shown about the house, and any one of them will tell you that the place is haunted. Infrequent ships still pass the house like phantoms from the great days, outward bound in lumber, and pass in with coffee and molasses. But no rum, and if Benning Wentworth knows, he is where he cares not. There is still some codfish—but it is dry, and salty.

When Washington came to Portsmouth he was of course entertained and fully instructed on the resources of the section. A part of the ceremonial of his reception was a fishing expedition. In his diary he complains of his luck. A band was blaring in his honor, and every fish in that portion of the Atlantic had retreated beyond the Isles of Shoals. A rod and line was handed to the general, and instantly he felt a tug. Up came twelve pounds of glittering cod. Huzzas from the crowd, congratulations for the chief, uproar from the band.

A canny fisherman, before yielding the rod to Washington, had quietly attached the fish to the hook. Was there ever nicer hospitality?

THE PRINGLE HOUSE

THE PRINGLE HOUSE

Royal governors have visited here; invading generals have made the house headquarters in two wars; it was twice besieged; a famous beauty left its doors and was lost at sea; and even Josiah Quincy was impressed by its hospitality. But there are new roses every springtime on the garden wall. . . .

THE PRINGLE HOUSE

IF tradition has any influence upon its own children, your true Charlestonian should be a violently proud person, who votes with a flourish, as a Signer would vote; who looks aloft—not at the sun—but at the spires of St. Michael's and St. Philip's, and seeing them in their proper places in Charleston's profile, knows that the world again revolves; who makes horrid faces regularly in the direction of Fort Sumter; who cheers "Huzza!" at the lightest mention of General Francis Marion; in short, who conducts himself generally in an extremely historic manner.

He has none of these gestures. He dines at mid-afternoon, goes amiably about his affairs, is aristocratic to a degree and in the same degree is gracefully hospitable. In the center of one of our country's most fertile areas of dramatic action he is not theatrical. It bothers you, for example, if he happens to be a Prioleau and you are passing the Huguenot church which a Prioleau founded in 1685, that he has no appropriate expression of Seventeenth Century piety.

If Charleston really knew what was expected of her in dramatic ritual she would do all those things. Happily Charleston does not know, or she might exploit and become odious. Instead she watches the cloth-of-gold roses climb the courtyard wall and is much more concerned with the forthcoming blossoms than with the ancestor who planted the roots. She has a back-drop as glorious as an old tapestry, but it is hung where it belongs—back. She attends St. Michael's and St. Philip's for today's devotions and tomorrow's salvation, which are the richer for yesterday's haunting footsteps. And only Charleston can truly appreciate—though the rest of the nation may admire and cherish—the old square house in King Street whose red-brick walls and shining white portico are framed by ancient trees at the curbing; the house Miles Brewton built; the house Charleston knows as the "Pringle House."

Miles Brewton was not primarily a soldier. His father and his grandfather had been for forty years custodians of gunpowder in Charles Town, but the colony's preliminary fighting had mostly been done by that time. When the combined forces of the Kings of France and Spain were driven out of the harbor forever in 1706, the colonists settled back to a half-century of peaceful commerce. The powder magazine on Cumberland Street was not often called upon to repel the invader, and the powder receiver's duties, though honorable service, were not over-exacting.

So Miles came into the dual inheritance of a quiescent military tradition and an active fortune. Naturally enough, since he had just married Miss Mary Izard, his thoughts turned on building a house; his taste suggested a beautiful house; his wealth permitted a house which Josiah Quincy described as "superb, . . . said to have cost him 18,000 sterling."

Josiah Quincy, though a Bostonian, believed in seeing America first. He had a most illuminating journey. He had never realized that Charles Town, in the Carolinas, was the richest city south of Philadelphia, nor that here he was to find a spirit of resentment against British injustice as acute as that of his own people. "This town," he wrote, "makes a beautiful appearance as you come up to it and in many respects a magnificent one. I can only say in general that in grandeur, splendor of building, decorations, equipages, numbers, commerce, shipping, and indeed everything it far surpasses all I ever saw or ever expect to see in America." From a Quincy of Massachusetts this was the perfect tribute.

What prompted it? In his diary of March 8, 1773 he writes: "Dined with a large company at Miles Brewton's, Esq., a gentleman of very large fortune. . . . At Mr. Brewton's sideboard was very magnificent plate. A very fine bird kept familiarly playing about the room under our chairs and the table, picking up the crumbs, and perching on the window and sideboard." The bird was evidently the crowning touch to a panoply of culture and luxury such as he had scarcely anticipated among the outlanders. You may picture him, if you like, rising comfortably fortified with good cooking, at the end of a whole afternoon at the five-yard table; identifying with shrewd appraisal the excellent furniture which his host and hostess had picked up in England five years before; running a furtive proving finger over the carved woodwork which had also come across the Atlantic; knowing that the portrait of Miles Brewton on the wall was *good*, and knowing that another reason why it was good was because Sir Joshua Reynolds had done it. Though there were slaves in Boston at that time, you may conjecture that he tacitly disapproved of the substantial slave quarters across the courtyard—for he was the ancestor of a brilliant abolitionist. But for the architectural excellence of the interior, its carved woodwork, and its furnishings, he could have nothing but praise. And at the risk of invading the visitor's privacy you may follow him to the King Street gate as he departs, and you may perhaps catch the emphatic wag of his head, and hear his conclusive whisper: "These people know how! They have *atmosphere!* I am amazed!" He carried back to Boston the warm friendship of Miles Brewton and the firm conviction that Charles Town could be relied upon.

FAMOUS COLONIAL HOUSES

Miles Brewton had for ten years been a member of the Commons House of the Colonial legislature. He had watched the smouldering of a spirit which would break out in flame the next spring, had given wise counsel to the hot-heads, yielded nothing to injustice from London. Then Charles Town heard the shot fired round the world. The Provincial Congress met, voted to raise three regiments and a million dollars. Into the uproar sailed his Majesty's Ship *Scorpion*, bearing Lord William Campbell, to be the new colonial governor, apparently for no special qualification except that he had married Sarah Izard, of Charles Town. Miles Brewton made his wife's cousin and her governor-husband his guests at once, and when the Provincial Congress promptly stuck its verbal bayonets under the uncomfortable young Campbell's nose, His Lordship stayed up half the night wondering what he could do, and then called Miles Brewton out of bed to help settle the question.

A Committee of Safety presently supplanted the Provincial Congress, and Brewton became a member. We know of his value to the colony in trying to preserve equilibrium. Of what his service in war might have been we can never know. Josiah Quincy had been urging upon his friend the courtesy of a return visit. With Mrs. Brewton and the children he took ship to Philadelphia—and Miles Brewton and his family were lost at sea. Josiah Quincy lost a friend and the cause a level-headed patriot.

Although its builder was gone, and his direct line wiped out, the Brewton house remained. It was left jointly to his sisters, Mrs. Charles Pinckney and Mrs. Jacob Motte. It was Mrs. Motte's home while Parker and Clinton hammered at the city gates in 1776, and it requires no documentary evidence to conceive how that "very magnificent plate" on the Brewton sideboard shone at dinner the

THE PRINGLE HOUSE

night of August second—the night when the battered British fleet had sailed away, and the night when Captain Barnard Elliott read the Declaration of Independence to the soldiery and the cheering townsfolk.

There came a day, however, four years later when Sir Henry Clinton cut off the peninsula from the mainland, and forced the city to surrender. A conqueror likes to be comfortable, and Sir Henry and his staff camped down upon Mrs. Motte's thoroughly comfortable house. You will find, scratched into one of its white marble mantels, a crude sketch of a British frigate, and a portrait of the conqueror himself, done by a staff-officer. Mrs. Motte, at the commander's request, presided at table, but the lady was as wise as she was tactful—her three attractive daughters were behind barred doors in the garret—a knowing precaution against the notorious tendencies of Lord Rawdon, who succeeded Sir Henry Clinton. Other homes in the town fared less well: Mrs. C. C. Pinckney and her family were turned out bodily, and the families upon whom were quartered certain of the lesser invaders were made wretched indeed.

Charles Town endured and waited. In pleasant weather the enemy staff lounged in the deep-walled garden which reaches back of the Motte house to Legare Street; when winter forced them indoors there were gay dinners in the high-panelled dining-room, dinners attended by those of the citizenry who had "played safe" and England to win. The patriots wore brave smiles and old dresses. If you had been a sentry during those days you might have challenged a charming young woman with a pass through the lines to visit her plantation. If you had been a dutiful sentry you would have glanced into her carriage, to make sure she carried no contraband. If you had been an impertinent sentry you might have seen that she wore heavy boots

—but if she had smiled at you you would not have been impertinent. And naturally when she returned through the lines two or three days later and smiled graciously upon you as an old friend, how could you know that those boots were men's boots, and that they were now in the stirrups of some cavalier serving under Marion, the Swamp Fox? Or read behind her smile the secret that Marion's men that night would ride the harder, harass the British patrols outside more bitterly, make foreign tenure of the city less and less comfortable? That was the secret of the women of Charles Town.

A British officer caught Colonel Isaac Hayne after a brilliant capture he had effected within five miles of the city. They brought him in and condemned him to death as a spy, which he was not. The drawing-room of the Motte house saw another phase of Charles Town's women: heard their pleading for Hayne's life; saw Rawdon refuse. Then imprisoned Charles Town saw Martyr Hayne hanged and bitterness crystallized to hate. The same Mrs. Motte who had been an unwilling hostess to the British in town went in 1780 to her plantation "Mount Joseph," on the Congaree. The British seized and fortified it the next year and she was moved to a nearby farmhouse, so that Marion and "Light Horse Harry" Lee could lay siege to the property. When Lee suggested to her the destruction of her own home by fire-bearing arrows, she agreed heartily, and herself brought forth an East-Indian bow and arrows of great range. The good lady then watched the marksmanship of Marion's men set fire to her own plantation house, applauded its surrender, and when the fire was out presided over captor and captive at her own table!

A watchman's cry put an end to the poverty and distress in which the besieged city found itself slowly mired. Cutting through the rain it brought candle-light to life in every house as the news spread:

THE PRINGLE HOUSE

"Half-past-twelve of a stormy night and Cornwallis has surrendered!" It meant victory, an end to suffering, reunited families. In 1782 Moultrie led his troops into the city, past "the balconies, the doors and windows crowded with the patriotic fair, the aged citizens and others congratulating us on our return home, saying, 'God bless you, gentlemen! You are welcome home, gentlemen!' Both citizens and soldiers shed mutual tears of joy."

For ten years the Motte house followed the city's returning prosperity. Of the three girls who had been hidden in the attic during the wretched Rawdon's incumbency, one, who married Thomas Pinckney, died young; the second, whose first husband died, married Pinckney and lived to see him the first American ambassador to England and a candidate for president. The third, Mary Brewton Motte, married William Alston, a colonel in Marion's Brigade.

It was natural, therefore, when President Washington journeyed to South Carolina in 1791, he should stop at Clifton, Colonel Alston's plantation, and marvel at the luxurious cultivation of the fields of young rice. If Mary Motte Alston had her mother's character and charm—as she probably did—it is no wonder the President who was also a good farmer told her the plantation "looked like fairyland." In his journal he wrote: "Went to a concert where were 400 ladies, the number and appearance of which exceeded anything I had ever seen." And later this: "Was visited about two o'clock by a great number of most respectable ladies in Charleston, the first honour of the kind I had ever experienced, as flattering as singular." Nor can we omit the fact that Commodore Gillon solved the delicate problem of where to seat the President at the state dinner by placing him opposite the loveliest lady in Charleston, and *next* to the wittiest.

In 1791 Colonel Alston bought the Motte house. As the Alston house it presided over the rise of an Alston to the governorship of the state. Its gate swung wide at the arrival in Charleston of Joseph Alston's second wife, Theodosia Burr. Theodosia sailed for New York in 1813 in the swift privateer, *Patriot*, to join her lonely father Aaron. Four weeks later Joseph Alston sat down at a French secretary in the drawing-room and wrote Burr, "I have in vain endeavored to build upon the hope of long passage. Thirty days are decisive. My wife is *either captured or lost.* What a destiny is mine!" The ship was never heard of again. Mrs. St. Julien Ravenel in her excellent volume, "Charleston, the Place and Its People," tells of the death-bed confession of an old sailor thirty years later, who had been one of a crew of pirates who had captured the ship and made the passengers walk the plank, and some color is given to this solution by an anonymous note found in a volume of Burr's letters, saying "Some account appeared in the New Orleans papers about 1848 of the deposition of a coloured woman—'in relation to the death of Mrs. Alston occasioned by Pirates.'"

The eldest daughter of the Alston house, born to the purple, justified her claim to it by marrying Robert Y. Hayne, some time Governor of South Carolina, United States Senator, and proprietor of the loser's share of a magnificent debate with Daniel Webster. That rare old gentleman, William Alston, lived until 1839. He was a practical planter who believed "that in the management of slaves the true interests of the planter were in exact accordance with the dictates of an enlightened humanity." He loved horses, maintained a good stable on the King Street place, and raced them in lively competition; this leads Mr. Huger Smith, in his neighborly story of the Alston house, to "wonder whether Washington's well known interest in such things led to the presence, at Colonel Alston's plantation in 1799,

THE PRINGLE HOUSE

of *Great Plenipo*, sired 'by *Royal Gift*, a Jack Ass presented to the late President Washington by the King of Spain.'—*Georgetown Gazette, April 17, 1799*." Certain it is that he owned *Betsy Baker*, who defeated Colonel William Washington's *Rosetta* in a stirring race, and *Gallattin*, and *Alborae*—famous turf names all.

His children made him happy, and he endeared himself to an army of friends, not the least of whom was Thomas Jefferson. It was Jefferson, the founder of the political party which has since committed prohibition, who wrote Colonel Alston in 1818:

> "I have therefore made up a box of a couple of doz. bottles among which you will find samples of the wines of White Hermitage, Ledanon, Rousillon (of Riveralto). Bergasse, claret, all of France and of Nice, and Montepulciano, of Italy."

The visitor who penetrates to that cellar today will find it empty.

But on the drawing-room walls he will find another letter from Jefferson—as he will find one from George Washington, both addressed to John Julius Pringle, and asking him to be attorney-general of the United States. Those letters hang there because John Julius Pringle, a great lawyer, had a son, William Bull Pringle, and because fate married him to Mary Motte Alston, and because she inherited the house—and the letter—from the fine old Colonel in 1839. His brother, Robert Pringle, was in Paris when the royal family abdicated, and had the opportunity to buy the chairs from Louis Philippe's palace which are such an ornament to the house today. Those letters from two presidents of the United States were cherished possessions of the family when another Robert Pringle was killed at Battery Wagner on Morris Island in the defense of his city against the United States. The teardrops of the crystal chandelier in that same drawing-room tinkled at the shock of two hundred and eighty days' firing upon Fort Sumter, while the harassed family lived through a bitter repetition of the siege of eighty-odd years before, and when the Federal troops occupied the city in 1865 history repeated itself as they made headquarters in the Pringle house. Fifty thousand suns have not faded the Indian dyes in the silk damask curtains Miles Brewton imported for his new house, nor have the sea-fogs dulled the French secretary that was Rebecca Motte's. Her high-boy is there today, so is a graceful and inviting old sofa. Time apparently cannot affect them—except as it makes these possessions infinitely more precious to the present gracious owners, Miss Susan Pringle Frost and her sisters. A seven-yard table cloth, for example, would be an exploit in linen even if it were dated 1921; dated, in scarlet cross-stitch, "Alston, 1797," Miss Frost's seven-yard table cloth is beyond price.

I have no doubt that when, in 1918, there were rumors of an enemy submarine base in the West Indies, and the possibility of raids upon Charleston seemed more than mere fancy, the Spirit of the House smiled, and whispered: "I recollect Miles Brewton's father telling of Blackbeard, the pirate. He was going to raid Charles Town, but thought better of it. Then Stede Bonnet—we *caught* him. There have been a lot of them, trouble-makers of one kind and another. Admiral Cervera and the Spanish had some such notion. Submarines? M-m-m, perhaps. Who knows? I'm going to take a little nap now, but if you want me, Charleston, let me know. I'll be about anyway when they commence to shell the town."

APPENDIX

THOSE who find in the stories of Mount Vernon and The Quincy Homestead a stimulus for the preservation of other famous American residences will naturally inquire into the successful methods of the organizations of patriotic women who now carry on that work in a manner so perfectly suited to the charge.

To answer those inquiries, and more particularly to record the identity of those who are now "carrying on," there follows a list of the current officers of the Mount Vernon Ladies' Association of the Union:

Regent

Miss Harriet Clayton Comegys
    On the Green, Dover, Delaware

Hon. Vice-Regent

Mrs. Elizabeth B. A. Rathbone	Michigan

Vice-Regents

Miss Alice M. Longfellow	Massachusetts
Mrs. Charles Custis Harrison	Pennsylvania
Mrs. Thomas S. Maxey	Texas
Mrs. Robert D. Johnston	Alabama
Mrs. Eugene Van Rensselaer	West Virginia
Mrs. John Julius Pringle	South Carolina
Mrs. William F. Barret	Kentucky
Mrs. Henry W. Rogers	Maryland
Miss Mary F. Failing	Oregon
Mrs. Eliza F. Leary	Washington
Mrs. J. Carter Brown	Rhode Island

APPENDIX

Vice-Regents

Mrs. James Gore King Richards	Maine
Miss Mary Evarts	Vermont
Mrs. Antoine Lentilhon Foster	Delaware
Miss Annie Ragan King	Louisiana
Miss Jane A. Riggs	District of Columbia
Mrs. Horace Mann Towner	Iowa
Mrs. Thomas P. Denham	Florida
Miss Harriet L. Huntress	New Hampshire
Mrs. Charles Eliot Furness	Minnesota
Mrs. Benjamin D. Walcott	Indiana
Mrs. Lucien M. Hanks	Wisconsin
Miss Annie Burr Jennings	Connecticut
Mrs. Willard Hall Bradford	New Jersey
Mrs. Charles Nagel	Missouri
Mrs. George A. Carpenter	Illinois
Miss Mary Govan Billups	Mississippi
Mrs. John V. Abrahams	Kansas
Mrs. Margaret Busbee Shipp	North Carolina
Mrs. Horton Pope	Colorado
Mrs. Charles J. Livingood	Ohio
Mrs. Randolph Anderson	Georgia
Mrs. Celsus Price Perrie	Arkansas
Mrs. Horace Van Denenter	Tennessee
Mrs. Charles S. Wheeler	California

The restoration and custody of The Quincy Homestead is in the hands of a committee of the Massachusetts Society of Colonial Dames. The promoting and sustaining figure in the work is the present chief executive of the Society, Mrs. Barrett Wendell, of Boston.

www.ingramcontent.com/pod-product-compliance
Lightning Source LLC
Chambersburg PA
CBHW081837170426
43199CB00017B/2756